365
GAMES
to make and play

365
GAMES
to make and play

Written by Jac Remise
English version by Jane Reid
Photographs by Frédéric and Jac Remise

First published in this edition 1979
Published by Octopus Books Limited
59 Grosvenor Street, London W1.
ISBN 0 7064 1055 6

Printed in Czechoslovakia
50389

Preface

Boxes of matches, corks, clothes-pegs, ping-pong balls . . . all these can be made into hundreds of toys and games. All children love small things and perhaps, most of all, they love little things that they have made for themselves. Most of these toys and games can be made by any deft-fingered child of seven or more, although some of them would need the help of an adult.

Each toy or game is illustrated with a full colour photograph of the finished project. Study these carefully before you begin to make them and then read the list of materials and the step-by-step instructions

Usually the games and toys are painted after they have been assembled but occasionally it is easier to paint the parts before they are glued together; this is always stated in the instructions.

For the adult and child this book is a treasure-trove of ideas both for whiling away a rainy afternoon or for making inexpensive but very attractive presents.

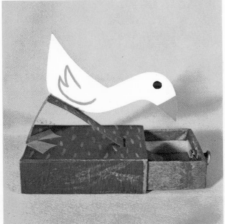

READ THIS FIRST . . .

Basic materials

Make a collection of these materials:
Empty matchboxes
Used matches
Drawing pins
Hairpins
Small nails
Pins
Rubber bands
Cardboard
Drawing paper
Corks
Toothpaste caps
Empty pill tubes
Sewing thread, wool and embroidery silks
Plasticine
Pine cones
Ping-pong balls
Drinking straws
Scraps of felt
Wooden cotton reels
String
Eggshells
Fuse-wire
Beads
Small boxes
Old light bulbs
Safety pins
Dried leaves and seeds
Nutshells
Clothes-pegs
Paper fasteners

Basic tools

You will need most of these:
Scissors
A sharp knife
A light hammer
A pair of pliers with a cutting notch
A gimlet
A hacksaw
A bodkin or a large darning needle
Crayons or felt pens
Water colours or poster paints
Brushes
A needle and thread
Varnish
Rubber solution glue
Paper adhesive
A pencil
A ruler
Graph paper
A pair of compasses

Preparing to make the toys and games

First wash your hands — this sounds such a simple thing but you will find that your models will look so much better if you keep them clean and always wash your hands after using glue or paint.

Protect your working surface with first, a thick sheet of cardboard or even a thin sheet of wood; (if you use a knife to cut or score paper it can easily damage the table). Cover the protective sheet with a double layer of newspaper.

Keep all the cutting tools together, all the glue together and all the paints together. Keep all spare materials away from the working area.

Wash your paintbrushes often and keep the pot of water where it will not be knocked over.

When you put aside newly painted models to dry, make sure that you will not touch them accidentally and so smudge them.

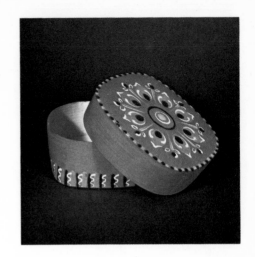

Making the patterns

You will find that many of the games use a pattern; since there is not room to give a full sized pattern these are sometimes very much reduced. This is what to do when you need to enlarge a pattern: The new size of the pattern is shown by the little centimetre key, for example:

15 mm
¾in

Draw a one centimetre grid over the pattern and then on a separate piece of paper draw a larger grid with the squares measuring the amount stated by the little key (as in the example above, the larger grid would have squares of 15mm.)

Now copy the pattern onto the larger grid, square for square.

Cut out the shape on the larger grid and use it as a trace shape.

Where there is no little centimetre key by a pattern this means that the pattern is the correct size already.

Cutting and scoring

Cutting corks:
Place the cork on the protected surface and put the blade of the knife parallel to the flat edge. Roll the cork back and forth under the knife while pressing down on the blade. This will give you a clean and even cut.

Cutting ping-pong balls:
If you heat the blade of the knife in a candle flame — CAREFULLY! — the knife will cut through the ping-pong ball easily.

Scoring:
Run the blunt side of the knife along the edge of a ruler placed along the line which needs to be scored.

Making holes:
Make holes in paper or card with a pin or a small nail (do this on a hard surface and where you won't damage the furniture!).

Make holes in pegs or corks by piercing them with a fine gimlet or darning needle, then with a small nail. Ping-pong balls can be pierced with a darning needle which has been gently heated in a candle flame — CAREFULLY!

Cutting out:
Cut paper and card with scissors and wood with a small hacksaw — CAREFULLY!

Cut wire or hairpins with the pliers.

CAUTION
Whenever you cut anything, ALWAYS CUT AWAY FROM YOURSELF.

If you are using candles or very sharp knives work with an adult.

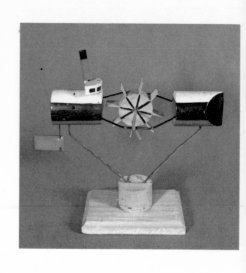

CONTENTS

119	Artificial Flowers	163	Two-Masted Yacht	202	Puppet with Hat
120	Watering-Can	164	Wind Racer	203	Musician
121	Garden Furniture	165	Submarine	204	Drummer
122	Flower Barrow	166	Sailor	205	Little Theatre
123	Hairdresser's Table	167	Galleon	206	Singer
124	Doll's Lamp	168	Three-Masted Ship	207	Weight Lifter
125	Ballet Dancer	169	Steamboat	208	Trumpeter
126	Costume Doll	170	Torpedo Boat	209	Guitarist
127	Table and Chair	171	1830 Paddle Boat	210	Dimitri the Dancer
128	Cradle	172	1920 Submarine	211	Ballroom Dancer
129	Chest of Drawers	173	Showboat	212	Musical Needles
130	Magazine Tidy	174	Growing Tree	213	See saw
131	Baby's Bed	175	Pocket Submarine	214	Accordion Player
132	Rag Doll	176	Saluting Sailor	215	Butterfly Catcher
133	English Gig	177	Wolf Mask	216	Egg Timer
134	Four Drawers	178	Tiny 'Plane	217	Semaphore Sailor
135	Farm	179	Three Speedboats	218	Patience Game, Little Baby
136	Skipping Rope	180	Tent	219	Paper Daisy
137	Father Christmas	181	Marble Game	220	Jumping Doll
138	Lamp	182	Timer	221	Balancing Act
139	Christmas Salt and Pepper	183	Boat	222	Telephone
140	Christmas Tree	184	Binoculars	223	Paddle Boat
141	Letter Sticker	185	Whaler	224	Little Liner
142	Calendar	186	Buoy	225	Montgolfier Balloon
143	Growing Snake	187	Grinding Mill	226	Unicyclist
144	Blue Telephone	188	Street Lamp	227	Fisherman
145	Growing Giraffe	189	Rodeo Rider	228	Gymnast
146	Egghead	190	Badminton Game (1)	229	Little Mermaid
147	Little Cinema	191	Badminton Game (2)	230	Acrobatic Clown
148	Photograph Frame	192	Hula-Hoop Game	231	Talking Bird
149	Magic Lantern	193	Chickens Picture	232	Lumberjacks
150	Flower Pot	194	Painted Egg (2)	233	Little Swimmer
151	Rocking Chair	195	Dancing Chicken Picture	234	Fencers
152	Television	196	Hostess	235	Sand Racer
153	Aircraft Carrier	197	Rubber Band Game	236	Weight Lifter (2)
154	Flag Carrier	198	Patience Game, Little Car	237	Kitchen Timer
155	Paddle Steamer	199	Racket and Ball Game	238	Medallion
156	Cork Pageboy	200	Yo-yo	239	Snail Glove Puppet
157	Marine Fire Tender	201	Ball and Cone Game	240	Flower Holder
158	1925 Ferry Boat			241	Small Photo-Frame
159	1950 Cargo Boat			242	Moving Snail
160	1960 Aircraft Carrier			243	Happy Clown
161	1930 Liner			244	Little Imp
162	1950 Tanker				

1 Steam Engine

You will need:

An empty tin, washed and dried, two circles of stiff card, each 60mm (2½in.) diameter, an oblong piece of card, 115 × 55mm (4½ × 2½in.) Two small corks, two rounds cut from a large cork, two used matches, a large hairpin, a narrow tube (sometimes pills or cigars come in suitable tubes), paint, brushes, glue, scissors

What to do:

Stick the can to the oblong piece of card, 15mm (¾in.) from the front, narrow edge of the card

Stick the two large circles of card to the sides of the tin as shown in the photograph

Stick the narrow tube to the front of the tin to make the chimney

Support the chimney with the hairpin

Stick the two rounds of cork to the sides of the card to make the back wheels as shown in the photograph

Push a match into each of the little corks

Stick the corks to the top edge of the back wheels

Paint the engine

The Driver

You will need:

A wooden clothes-peg, two used matches, a cap from a toothpaste-tube, a small scrap of paper (for the brim of the driver's cap), a 15mm (¾in.) circle of card, paint, brushes, glue, scissors

What to do:

Remove the wire clip from the peg and turn the halves of the peg back-to-back so that the flat sides are together. Glue them together

Stick the matches on to make arms

Cut a crescent-shaped brim for the cap and stick the toothpaste-tube cap to the brim

Stick the completed cap to the rounded ends of the joined pegs

Paint the engine driver

Stick the engine driver to the circle of card and then stick the card circle to the base of the engine as shown in the photograph

2 The Tender

You will need:

The drawer from a large box of matches, four rounds cut from a large cork, about fifteen little pebbles painted black, glue, paint, scissors, brushes, ruler

What to do:

Carefully make a triangular cut at one end of the matchbox drawer so that the short end is free from the sides of the box but still attached at the base

Measure along the long sides for 70mm (2¾in.) from the cut end, cut the box off at this point

Stick the free end of the box to the diagonal cut to make the third side of the tender

Glue on the rounds of cork to make the wheels

Paint the tender

Fill it with the little pebbles

3 Carriage

You will need:

A medium-sized box of matches, four rounds cut from a large cork, a strip of drawing paper large enough to cover the matchbox twice. Paint, brushes, glue, scissors, ruler

What to do:

Separate the two parts of the matchbox and glue them together, narrow side to narrow side

With the cover at the bottom, trim the lower edge of the cover into a curve, trim both sides

Use the shape of the two parts of the matchbox as a pattern and cut out two pieces of paper to cover the sides of the carriage

Glue the paper to the carriage so that the open side of the matchbox drawer is covered

Stick the rounds of cork to the base of the carriage

Paint the carriage

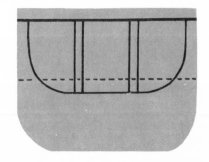

4 Signals

You will need:

Three crayons or pencils, one round piece of card 65mm (2½in.) in diameter, one square piece of card 70 × 70mm (2¾ × 2¾in.), two strips of card 105 × 20mm (4 × ¾in.), three circles of card 65mm (2½in.) in diameter, paint, brushes, glue

What to do:

Colour the signs as shown in the photograph

Stick the signs to the sharpened end of the crayons

Glue the other ends of the pencils to the card circles so that they will stand steadily

35 mm
1½in

5 Acrobatic Elephant

You will need:

A small box of matches, a paper fastener, drawing paper, paint, brushes, pencil, scissors, glue

What to do:

Trace the elephant from the pattern below, onto a piece of drawing paper

Paint it

Fold along the dotted lines of the base and cut the front foot away from the front pedestal

Attach point A to the front of the matchbox drawer with the paper-fastener

Glue the other end of the strip (B) to the top of the matchbox

Open and close the matchbox very gently to make the elephant move

15 mm
¾in

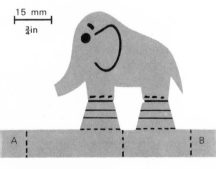

A   B

6 The Viaduct

You will need:

Two covers from small matchboxes, four used matches, a strip of card 200 × 23mm (8 × ⅞in.), paint, brushes, glue, scissors

What to do:

Cut the two matchbox covers into the shapes shown below

Stick the card strip into place

Stick the matches into place (see the photograph)

Paint the viaduct

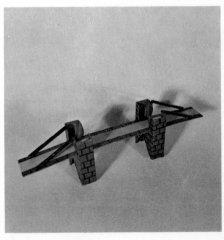

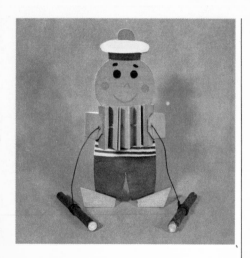

7 Sailor with a Squeezebox

You will need:

Cardboard, drawing paper, an elastic band, button thread, two small twigs, paint, brushes, glue, scissors

What to do:

Cut out the body (1) and the arms (2) of the sailor from the card

Cut out the squeezebox (3) from the drawing paper

Make little holes in the pieces where they are marked with a cross

Paint all the pieces

Fold them along the dotted lines

Stick piece 2 (the arms) behind the body of the sailor

Thread the elastic band through the holes in the squeezebox and tie a little thread to each end

Tie the ends of the thread to the twigs

8 Drum Major

You will need:

A wooden clothes-peg, two used matches, a small cork, a round piece cut from a cork, a piece of paper, a glass headed pin, a bead, a length of wire, glue, scissors, paint, brushes

What to do:

Remove the wire clip from the peg and turn the halves of the peg back to back. Glue them together

Saw off the curved top of the pegs at the level of a hat brim

Make a hollow in the round of cork and glue the pointed ends of the pegs into it

Stick the matchsticks on to make arms

Stick the wire into the base-cork and glue it to the right arm

Stick the bead to the top of the wire

Stick the small cork to the sawn off top of the pegs

Make a peak for the helmet with a semi-circle of paper

Stick the glass-headed pin onto the cork

Paint the drum major

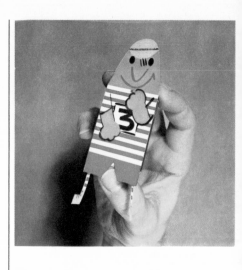

9 Olympic Walker

You will need:

A small matchbox, half of a matchstick, drawing paper, scissors, paint, brushes

What to do:

Copy the body and legs of the walker onto the drawing paper

Paint them

Remove the base from the drawer of the box of matches

Stick the body of the walker onto the front of the matchbox cover. (The top of his T-shirt should reach the top of the matchbox)

Stick a leg to the lower sides of the hollow matchbox drawer

30 mm
1¼in

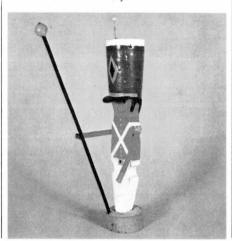

15 mm
¾in

Pierce a hole in the walker's throat

Push the half match through the hole and let it rest on both top edges of the matchbox cover with the hollow matchbox drawer resting on the match

Paint the Olympic walker

Hold the walker as shown in the photograph and rock the hollow matchbox drawer to make the legs move

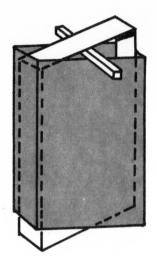

10 Pageboy

You will need:

A wooden clothes-peg, a round from a large cork, two used matches, a cap from a pill tube, paint, brushes, scissors

What to do:

Remove the wire clip from the peg and turn the halves of the peg back-to-back so that the flat sides are together

Glue them together

Cut a small groove into the round of cork and stick the base of the pegs into it

Stick the used matches into place for the arms

Stick the cap of the pill tube in place on the rounded heads of the pegs

Paint the pageboy

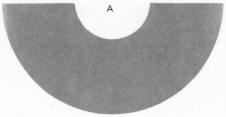

A

11 Local Train

You will need:

A small box of matches, a cork, two rounds of cork, two used matches, drawing paper, two small tops from pill tubes or little bottles, scissors, paint, brushes, glue

What to do:

Cut the two rounds of cork in half,

Stick the four semi-circles of cork onto the matchbox cover so that they look like wheels

Stick a used match onto each side to look like a piston rod

Stick the cork to the matchbox cover to make the boiler

Cut the matchbox drawer to make the driver's cab. The drawing below shows you how to do this

Stick the cab in place

Stick the caps from the pill tubes or bottles onto the boiler to make the chimneys

Cut out the drawing paper into the shape shown in pattern A. Curl this up and stick it to the front chimney

Paint the train

The Tender

You will need:

The drawer from a box of matches, two rounds cut from a cork, glue, paint, brushes, scissors

What to do:

Make two slanting cuts at one end of the matchbox drawer

Stick the end of the matchbox to the slanted sides

Cut the two rounds of cork in half and stick the four halves to the base of the matchbox drawer to make the wheels

Paint the tender

12 Passenger Wagon

You will need:

Three little boxes of matches, two rounds cut from a cork, glue, paint, brushes

What to do:

Stick the three matchboxes together

Cut the rounds of cork in half and glue them to the base of the wagon

Paint the wagon

13 Goods Wagon

You will need:

The drawer from a box of matches, two rounds cut from a cork, four used matches, glue, paint, brushes

What to do:

Cut the rounds of cork in two and stick them to the base of the matchbox drawer to make the wheels

Cut two of the matches in half and stick the halves into each corner of matchbox drawer

Stick the whole matches across the top of the half matches to make the rails for the wagon

Paint the wagon

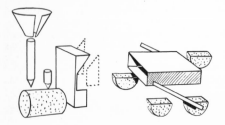

14 Wagon with a Canopy

You will need:

A box of matches, four used matches, two rounds cut from a cork, paint, scissors, glue, brushes

What to do:

Separate the drawer and the cover of the matchbox

Cut the cover into the canopy shape (the little diagram shows) what shape to make)

Cut the rounds of cork in half and stick them onto the base of the box

Stick a used match in each corner and stick the canopy on top of them

Paint the wagon

15 Little Blacksmith

You will need:

A small box of matches, drawing paper, scissors, a pencil, paint, brushes

What to do:

Draw the blacksmith onto the drawing paper

Paint him

Cut him out, fold along the dotted lines

Separate the hammer and the anvil

Stick point A to the box and point B to the drawer

To make the blacksmith work, move the drawer of the box gently in and out

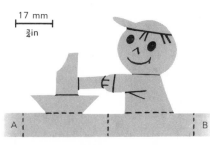

17 mm
¾in

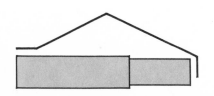

16 Mexican with Pony

You will need:

A small box of matches, drawing paper, a small piece of india rubber, scissors, a pencil, paint, brushes, a small pin

What to do:

Cut them out and fold them along the dotted lines

Stick the base of the horse to the matchbox

Stick point B on the Mexican to the matchbox drawer

Push the pin through the Mexican at point D and through the horse at point C. The little Mexican will now be sitting on the horse

Hold the pin in place and protect the point with the little piece of india rubber

When you push the matchbox drawer in and out gently the little Mexican will ride his horse

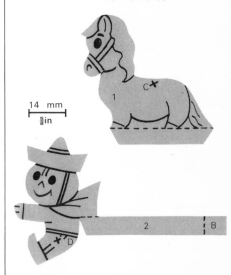

14 mm
⅝in

17 Small Racing Car

You will need:

Seven half ping-pong balls, a round cut from a cork, thin wire, 10 beads, a toothpaste-tube cap, 5 pins, drawing paper, cardboard, scissors, paint, glue, brushes, pencil

What to do:

Cut 5 rounds from the cardboard, each round should cover the open side of a half ping-pong ball

Cut out shape B from the cardboard, this is the underneath of the car

Cut out shapes C and D from drawing paper

Roll piece D so that it curves in the middle of the long edges. Roll this round the ping-pong ball which forms the seat and stick the ends to the sides of the last half ping-pong ball

Stick the cockpit to the pointed end of piece B making sure that when the engine cover is in place it will butt up against the windscreen

Stick the engine-cover onto the radiator ping-pong ball as well as the front of the windscreen and the sides of the base piece

Push a length of wire through the bonnet at the point where the front wheels will be placed

Place two beads on each end of the wire and then a wheel. Twist the ends of the wire to hold the wheels in place

Push another length of wire through the back of the racing car to make the axle for the back wheels

Put three beads onto each end and then the back wheels. Twist the wire to hold the wheels in place

Paint the car

18 Sledge

You will need:

Two halves of a wooden peg, the drawer from a small matchbox, two half-matches, glue, paint, brushes, varnish

What to do:

Glue the matchbox drawer to the two half-pegs as shown in the picture

Glue the two half-matches into the matchbox drawer to make the handle

Paint and varnish the sledge

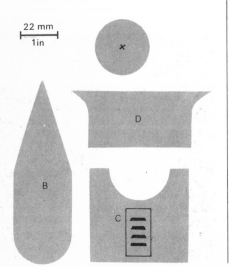

22 mm
1in

B

D

C

19 School Bus

You will need:

A box from a 120 photographic film, a large hairpin, 4 little tyres from an old toy car, a cork, glue, scissors, paint, brushes, pliers

What to do:

Open the single flap at one end of the box, fold the little side flaps diagonally so that they make sloping sides to support the larger flap

Glue the larger flap in place

Carefully open the flaps and the other end of the box, cut off the underneath flaps. The two flaps left will make the rear doors

Cut the hairpin into two pieces, each 4cm long

Push the wire pieces through the carton to form the axles of the bus

Cut four little circles from the cork to fit inside the tyres

Glue the little circles of cork in place

Push the wheels onto the ends of the hairpin axles and glue them in place

Paint the bus

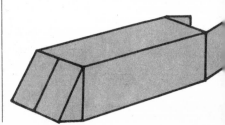

20 Scooter

You will need:

A cork, two rounds cut from a cork, four little eyelets, 2 matches, a small piece of red felt, drawing paper, a small piece of stiff transparent plastic, scissors, paint, brushes, glue

What to do:

Cut the cork in half lengthways and then cut one of the halves into half widthways

Glue one of the quarter corks to the half cork to make the body of the scooter

Push the eyelets into the sides of the seat as shown in the photograph

Cut a right-angled quarter out of each round of cork (these are the wheels) and glue them into place

Stick a match to the front wheel, cut out the front piece from drawing paper, stick this to the match with another match stuck across the top at right angles to make the handlebars

Stick the windscreen (cut from transparent plastic) to the handlebars

Cut the seat from felt and stick it in place

Paint the scooter

Windscreen

Front piece

Seat

21 Old Racing Car

You will need:

Six corks, a large hairpin, a drawing pin, three little caps from paint tubes, 18 pins, a straw, drawing paper, paint, brushes, scissors and glue, 2 wide rubber bands — to fit round the rounds of cork

What to do:

Assemble the racer in this order:

Radiator — half a round of cork with five pins stuck into it

Bonnet — two corks stuck end to end

Driving seat — a half-cork with a quarter cut away and a small strip of paper stuck in a V (see picture)

Back — a cork cut to a point and glued behind the seat

Front wheels — rounds of cork attached to the bonnet with pins

Back wheels — two rounds of cork with a wide rubber band round each, attached to the back of the racer with pins

Axle — a length of hairpin inside a length of drinking straw, glued diagonally between the front and back wheel

Lights and petrol cap — small caps from paint tubes stuck in place

Geat lever — 2 pins pushed into the side of the cockpit

Steering wheel — a drawing pin

Brake — a small length of drinking tube pinned to the side of the cockpit with two pins

Spare wheel — a round of cork pinned to the side of the bonnet

Windscreen — a small piece of drawing paper

Bonnet straps — two flat rubber bands

Paint the racing car

22 Rolling Ladybird

You will need:

A ping-pong ball, a cork, a large hairpin, scissors, paint, brushes, pliers

What to do:

Cut off the lower third of the ping-pong ball

Cut the cork so that it fits inside the ping-pong ball

Cut the hairpin in two

Use a part of the hairpin wire to make the axle for the cork 'wheel'

Push the wire through the side of the ping-pong ball and through the cork then through the other side of the ping-pong ball (see the diagram)

Paint the ladybird

If you place the ladybird on a slope it will roll down

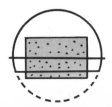

23 Veteran Car (1)

You will need:

Cardboard, two corks, a pin, three large hairpins, pliers, paint, brushes, a bead, a small nail which will go through the bead, scissors

What to do:

Cut out the parts of the body of the car from cardboard

1 Floor

2 Seats

3 Sides (cut two)

4 Steering wheel

Crease all the pieces along the dotted lines

Glue the sides of the car to the floor

Cut one of the corks in half lengthways and trim it so that the longest part fits at the front of the floor to make the bonnet and the smaller part fits between the back

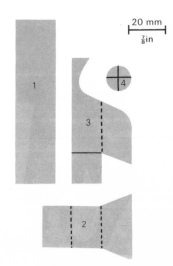

20 mm
$\frac{7}{8}$in

parts of the side to make the boot

Push the pin through the steering wheel and stick it to the cork of the bonnet

Bend one of the hairpins into the shape of the frame of the windscreen and push the ends into the bonnet

Cut the other hairpins in half and use two of the halves to make the axles and one other half for the starting handle

Make four wheels from the remaining cork and push the axles through to attach the wheels to the body

Make the radiator cap with the bead attached to the bonnet with the nail

Paint the car

24 Three-wheeled Car

You will need:

A ping-pong ball, a large hairpin, three little beads which will thread onto the hairpin, a pin, pliers, paints, brushes, scissors

What to do:

Cut off the lower third of the ping-pong ball

Cut the hairpin in two, one half makes the front axle with a bead at each end, the other half makes the back axle with the third bead making a wheel when threaded inside the ping-pong ball

Bend the ends of both axles to keep them in place

Push the pin into the top of the ping-pong ball and paint the car

25 Small Jeep

You will need:

Cardboard, two corks, a pin, three hairpins, scissors, paint, pliers, brushes

What to do:

Cut out the parts of the car from cardboard

1 Body

2 Seat

3 Wheel

Crease all the pieces along the dotted lines, stick A to A and B to B

Cut one of the corks in half lengthways and then trim it so that it fits on the front of the car (C)

Push the pin through the steering wheel and into the bonnet

Make one of the hairpins into the windscreen frame and push the ends into the bonnet

Use the other hairpins to make the axles and the starting handle

Cut the other cork into four wheels and attach these to the end of each axle

Paint the jeep

26 Little Bubble Car

You will need:

A ping-pong ball, a cork, a large hairpin, a pin, pliers, scissors, paint, paintbrush

What to do:

Cut off a third of the ping-pong ball

Cut the cork so that it will fit inside the ping-pong ball (see the diagram in project 22)

Cut the hairpin in two

Use one of the hairpin halves to make an axle for the cork 'wheel'

Push the wire through the side of the ping-pong ball and through the cork and then through the other side of the ping-pong ball

Paint the bubble car

If you place the bubble car on a slope it will run down

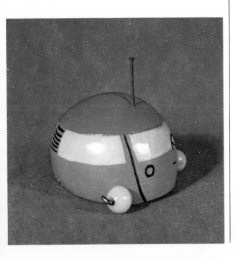

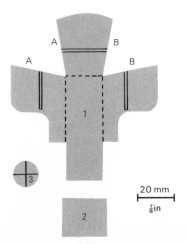

A   B

A   B

1

3

2

20 mm

$\frac{7}{8}$in

coloured picture

Trim the cork so that it will fit into the cut out hole on the cover of the matchbox

Push a pin through the centre of the cork and cut a slit in the top of the cork, cut off the sharp end of the pin

Insert the cork into the matchbox and push the boat's base into the slit in the top of the cork

Paint the boat

The base of the cork must touch the base of the matchbox drawer

When you gently push the matchbox drawer in and out the boat will rock

27 Sailing Boat

You will need:

A small box of matches made from cardboard, a cork, a pin, drawing paper, scissors, pliers, paint, brushes

What to do:

Cut out the three parts of the model from the plans below

Paint them (see the picture)

The black shapes in the centre of pieces 1 and 2 are cut away and a similar shape is cut out of the top of the matchbox cover

Glue first piece 1 onto the matchbox cover and then piece 2, matching up the holes. Fold the waves up as shown in the

28 Small Doll

You will need:

A very small bottle, a ping-pong ball, a length of green felt 12 cm × 2 cm (6 in. × 1 in.), glue, a small triangle of drawing paper, scissors, paint, brushes

What to do:

Stick the ping-pong ball to the neck of the bottle and paint a face onto it.

Paint a body onto the bottle.

When they are dry, wrap the strip of felt around the neck of the bottle and fringe its ends.

Stick the scarf in place

29 Conjurer

You will need:

A small matchbox, drawing paper, glue, paint, brushes, scissors

What to do:

Cut out the conjurer from the shape below

Bend along all the dotted lines

Stick B to the matchbox drawer and stick A to the matchbox sleeve

Paint the matchbox, the conjurer and the rabbit

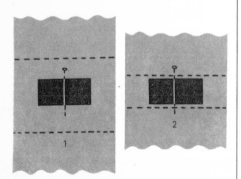

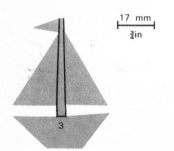

17 mm
¾in

15 mm
¾in

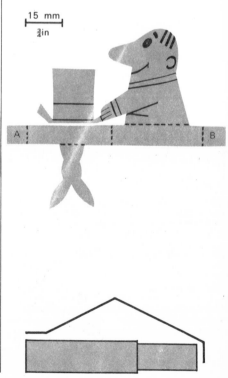

A   B

30 Polite Puppet

You will need:

A clothes-peg, a large hairpin, a drawing pin, a small piece of cork, a small nail, paint, brushes, glue, scissors, pliers, cardboard

What to do:

Cut the puppet and his arm out of cardboard

Paint them

Make a hole at each of the points A, B and C

Fold the piece of card D under and to the back of the puppet

Glue D to one side of the peg so that the puppet sits astride the peg

Cut the hairpin in half and twist it so that it resembles figure E

Pass the bent tip of the wire through hole C and fix the other end to the lower part of the peg with a drawing pin

Attach the arm of the puppet to the back of the puppet by pushing a pin through A and then B, protect the tip of the pin with a small piece of cork

Squeeze the peg to make the puppet raise and lower his hat

into the knot will keep the elastic
in place
Tie the other end of the elastic to
the front axle

Replace the top of the tube

Paint the racing car

Stick a pin into the front left-hand
wheel and wind the wheel round,
this will tighten the elastic and so
power the car

31 Old Racing Car

You will need:

A tube made of thin metal about
14cm (5½in.) long, a cork, a
matchstick, cardboard, two pieces
of wire each 9cm (4⅓in.) long, 4
beads with holes large enough for
the wire to pass through, elastic, a
pin, scissors, paint, brushes, pliers

What to do:

Cut four rounds of cardboard each
6cm (2½in.) in diameter, and a
windscreen 2cm × 2cm (¾in. ×
¾in.)

Make four holes in the metal tube
with a small nail, these are for the
axles

Make another hole in the base of
the tube (for the elastic)

Cut four rounds of cork and stick a
round to each cardboard circle

Push each wire axle through the
tube and put a bead on each end
of the axles

Push the wheels onto the end of
the axles

Thread the elastic through the hole
in the base of the tube and tie a
knot in the end of the elastic, a
small piece of matchstick inserted

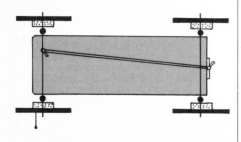

32 Cup and Ball Game

You will need:

Two ping-pong balls, two corks, a
length of thin string, a small nail,
paint, brushes, glue, varnish, a
darning needle

What to do:

Stick the corks together end to end

Cut one of the ping-pong balls in
half and fix one half to the corks
with a small nail

Tie one end of the string to the
nail, between the cork and the cup

Thread the needle with the free
end of the string and push the
needle through the other ping-
pong ball, tie a knot in the string
so that the ping-pong ball is held
onto the string

Paint and then varnish the cup and
ball game

33 Another Racing Car

You will need:

A cork, stiff drawing paper,
cardboard, two pieces of wire
each 8½cm (3⅓in.) long, 4 beads
through which the wire will pass,
two pins, elastic, paint, brushes,
scissors, pliers, glue

What to do:

Cut out the drawing paper to make
the body of the car (A)

Pierce it at the four points marked
on the plan

Roll the paper into a tube and
glue it

Lightly flatten the tube

Cut out the windscreen (B) and
stick it to the car-body

Cut four rounds of cork and four
circles of card each 3½cm (1½in.)
in diameter

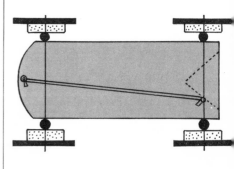

25 mm

1 in

Stick the cork rounds to the circles of cardboard

Push the wire axles through the car body

Place a bead on each end of the axles

Push a wheel onto each axle

Bend the axle ends over to hold the wheels in place

Push a pin into the front of the bonnet

Tie the elastic to this pin

Tie the other end of the elastic to the back axle

Paint the racing car

Gently wind up the back wheels to tighten the elastic

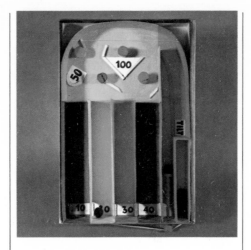

34 Flea Game

You will need:

A piece of cardboard 25cm × 25cm (10in. × 10in.), 4 corks, a saucer, 12 rounds of cork, 4 short lengths of flexible metal, scissors, paint, brushes, glue

What to do:

Cut a slit in each cork and push a flexible metal strip into each cork

Stick each cork onto one corner of the cardboard square

Paint the game

Place the saucer in the middle of the cardboard

To play the game you try to flick the cork rounds into the saucer using the metal strips as a springboard

35 Pinball Game

You will need:

A flat box, strips of cardboard, 7 little rounds of cork, used matches, a large rubber band, glue, scissors, paint, brushes

What to do:

Stick a long strip of cardboard round the inside of the box so that the top is curved

Stick four more strips of cardboard into the other end of the box, three of these should end $\frac{2}{3}$ of the way up the box and the fourth should be longer (see photograph)

In the right-hand compartment, stick a little strip of card, bent into a right-angle at the top to make a holder for spare beads

Stick the matches and 5 of the little rounds of cork onto the top third of the box to make the obstacles (see photograph)

Make a plunger by pushing a matchstick through the lower edge of the box and pushing a cork round onto each end

Place the large rubber band right round the outside of the box. This acts as the power for the plunger

Paint and varnish the game

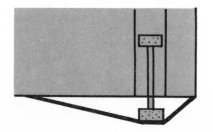

36 Starter Box

You will need:

The handle of an old paint brush, about 16cm (6in.) long, a cork, cardboard, a narrow box about 16cm (6in.) long and 5cm (2in.) square, a length of wire, paint, brushes, scissors

What to do:

Open one end of the box and make a hole in the other end

Wind the wire round a pencil to make a spring

Push the paintbrush handle through the hole and slip the spring round the handle

Push a cork onto the end of the handle stick a square of cardboard onto the cork (the diagram shows how the box is assembled)

Paint the starter box

The paintbrush handle acts as a catapult to push the car out of the starting-box

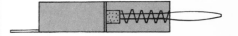

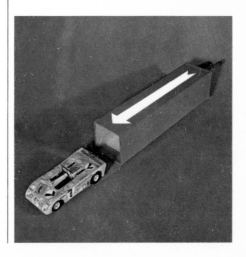

37 Veteran Car 1900

You will need:

A large box of kitchen matches, a cork, two small caps from toothpaste tubes, four beads, two lengths of wire, each 12cm (5in.) long, two used matches, two pins, an oval lamp bulb, drawing paper, scissors, glue, paint, brushes

What to do:

The chassis is made from the cover of the matchbox

Make a hole in the chassis to take the neck of the lamp bulb

Cut out two of each of pieces 3 and 4 and stick them onto the lamp bulb to make the arms and legs

Paint the little man

Push the two lengths of wire through the chassis (see diagram 1) to make the axles

Cut the cork into 4 rounds

Cut out four rounds of card for the wheels (figure 2)

Stick a round of cork to each round of card

Place a bead on each end of each axle and then push a completed wheel onto each axle end

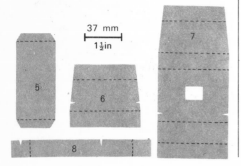

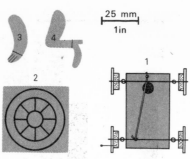

Tie the elastic to the back axle

Push a pin through the front of the chassis and tie the other end of the elastic to this

Stick the other pin into the back wheel to make a winding handle

Cut out the body of the car from the matchbox cover

The bonnet (5), the front (6), the hood (7) and the mudguards (8)

Stick the body onto the chassis

Stick two matches to the front to support the hood

Stick two tube caps to the front to make headlights

Paint the car

38 Letter Holder

You will need:

A wooden cotton reel, a cork, a peg, a hacksaw, paint, brushes, a small nail

What to do:

Saw off one end of the bobbin

Stick the cork to this

Place the peg on the cork and hold the peg in place with a small nail pushed through the spiral coil in the peg and into the cork

Paint the letter holder

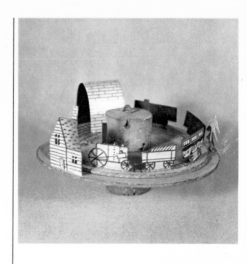

39 Historic Train

You will need:

A cork, a large hairpin, paper, scissors, paint, brushes, glue, stiff cardboard, paper

What to do:

Cut out the two circles shown on the next page, from stiff card

Cut out all the other shapes from drawing paper

Paint them

Cut the cork in half

Glue one half of the cork to the top of the small circle of card and the other half to the bottom of the large circle of card

Make a hole through both cork-halves and circles of card (1)

Straighten the hairpin and push it through the holes. Bend the ends of the hairpin over

Stick the house and one side of the tunnel to the large circle of card (the other side of the tunnel is not stuck down)

Stick the train on the rails on the smaller circle

The train will move if you rotate the smaller circle

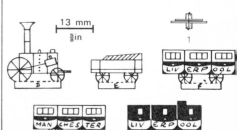

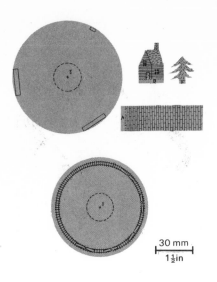

30 mm
1½in

40 French Policeman

You will need:

A wooden peg, a round of cork, three matches, drawing paper, scissors, glue, paint, brushes

What to do:

Separate the two halves of the peg and glue them together back-to-back

Make a slit in the cork round and push the pointed ends of the glued pegs into this

Cut out one sword, two hat-shapes and the moustaches from drawing-paper

Stick the hat and the moustaches to the pegs

Stick the matches to the pegs to make the arms

Stick the sword to the left arm

Paint the policeman

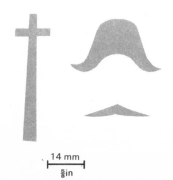

14 mm
⅝in

41 Old Racing Car

You will need:
A cork, an aluminium tube, two large hair pins, a pin, four beads, an elastic band, paint, brushes

What to do:
Cut off the curved end of the aluminium tube

Cut along the tube to open it

Nip one end of the tube to a slender point with a small opening underneath

Open the other end slightly (see diagram)

Push the pin through the slender end and tie the elastic to it

Straighten the hairpins to make the axles

Push each axle through the tube

Place a bead on each axle-end

Push a round of cork onto each axle-end

Trim the back axle

Bend one end of the front axle into a handle

Tie the loose end of the elastic to the front axle

Paint the racing car

42 Scooters

You will need:
(For each scooter) a large hairpin, a cork, paint, scissors, glue, brushes

What to do:
Cut each cork into three rounds

Use two rounds for the wheels

Cut the remaining round in half

Cut the hairpins in half

Join the wheels with a half-hairpin

Stick the half-round of cork between the wheels

Cut the remaining half-hairpin in half

Bend each half into a right-angle

Stick the right-angled pieces into the front wheel to make the handlebars

Paint the scooters

43 Small Racing Car

You will need:
A cork, 26cm of thin wire, (10½in.) 4 beads, three pins, 20cm (8in.) elastic, a cap from a small paint-tube, a straw, drawing paper, card, glue, scissors, paint, brushes

What to do:
Cut out two shapes of plan 1 and one of plan 2 from the card

Cut out plans 3 and 4 from drawing paper

Pierce shapes 1 at A, B, C and D

Stick the sides to the base and the bonnet to the sides and then the back of the car to the sides

Pin the straw to the side of the car to make the exhaust

Stick the paint-tube cap to the car to make the petrol cap

Push the axles (the wire cut in quarters) through the chassis at A, B, C and D and tie one end of the elastic to the front wire A

Pass the elastic round axle C and back to axle B, tie it to axle B

Cut the cork into four rounds

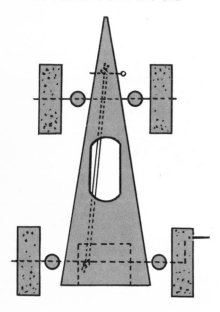

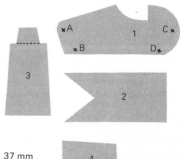

Cut four 3cm (1¼in. circles from card

Glue a cork round to each card circle

Place a bead at the ends of axles B and D

Push the wheels onto the axles

Push a pin into one of the front wheels to make a winding handle

45 Patience Game (Road Sign)

You will need:

The drawer of a little box of matches, a match, drawing paper, scissors, paint, brushes, glue, Cellophane

What to do:

Cut a rectangle of paper which will fit into the matchbox drawer

Draw a road sign on it with the base marked by dotted lines

Paint the sign

Stick the paper into the drawer

Cut the match in two

Paint each match half

Place the match halves in the drawer

Cover the open side of the drawer with Cellophane

46 Winch for Toy Car

You will need:

A piece of wood 9 × 20cm (3½ × 8in.), a cork, 50cm (20in.) wire, a safety-pin, a bead, two circles of card each 4cm (1¾in.) diameter, thread, a large elastic band, pliers, a bodkin, glue

What to do:

Cut the wire into three pieces, two of 20cm (8in.) and one of 10cm (4in.)

Bend the longer pieces into V shapes with a loop at the top of the V

Push the ends of the wire into the piece of wood

Glue the rounds of card to each end of the cork

Attach one end of the elastic band to the right hand wire V

Thread the band through the cork

Cut the remaining wire in half and make a handle with one half

Thread the bead onto the handle and push the handle into the cork through the loop on the left-hand V

Make a hook with the remaining wire and tie it to the thread, wind the thread round the cork after passing it through the spiral of a half safety-pin pushed into the wood

44 Warning Sign

You will need:

Half a cotton reel, half a pencil, a triangle of card with 5½cm (1in.) sides, a little saw, paint, brushes

What to do:

Push one end of the half-crayon into the hole in the centre of the bobbin

Saw a slit in the other end of the crayon

Push the triangle into the slit

Paint the sign

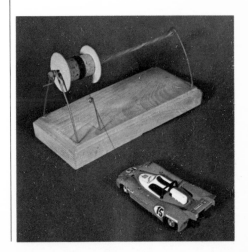

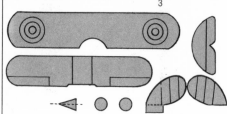

Stick the roundels to the side of
the peg

Use a small piece of the match to
make the propeller

Glue the 'plane to the box and
paint it. Varnish it when dry

47 French Fighter 'Plane

You will need:

A small box of matches, a used
match, a wooden peg, a hacksaw,
drawing paper, 4 drawing pins,
scissors, paint, brushes, a round of
cork, a pin

What to do:

Separate the halves of the peg

Trim one half of the peg as shown
in figures A, B, C and D

Push a drawing pin into the front
upper part of the peg and a pin
into the lower back of the peg
(see figure 2)

Push another drawing pin into the
nose of the 'plane

Cut out the wings, roundels and
tail pieces from drawing paper (3)

Glue the large wing to the top of
the peg and the smaller wing to
the lower side of the peg

Cut the round of cork into quarters
and glue one quarter to the peg to
make the undercarriage

Push 2 drawing pins into the cork
to make the wheels

Stick the tail to the 'plane

48 Space Capsule

You will need:

The neck part of a plastic bottle,
a cork, a large nail, card, glue,
scissors, paint, brushes

What to do:

Cut a round of card to cover the
open end of the bottle neck

Stick it in place

Push a cork into the small end of
the bottle neck

Push the nail into the cork

Paint the capsule

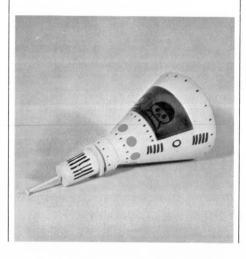

49 English Fighter 'Plane

You will need:

A small box of matches, a used
match, a wooden peg, a hacksaw,
drawing paper, 4 drawing pins,
scissors, paint, brushes, a round of
cork cut in quarters, a pin

What to do:

Separate the halves of the peg

Trim one half of the peg as shown
in figures A, B, C and D

Push a drawing pin into the upper
front part of the peg and a pin into
the lower back part of the peg

Cut out the wings, roundels, tail
piece and cockpit of the plane
from drawing paper (3)

Glue the large wing to the
drawing-pin on the top of the peg

Glue the small wing to the
underneath of the peg

Glue a quarter of the cork round to
the peg to make the undercarriage

Push two drawing pins into the
cork to make the wheels

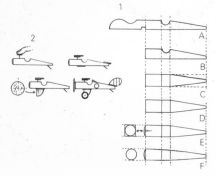

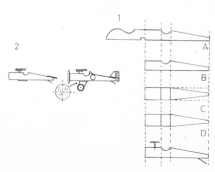

Stick the tail to the 'plane
Stick the roundels in place
Use a small piece of match to
make a propeller
Glue the 'plane to the matchbox
Paint and varnish it

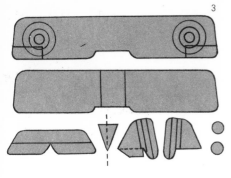

50 Saluting Soldier

You will need:
A peg, two matches, a round of
cork, drawing paper, a cap from a
small tube, scissors, brushes, paint,
glue

What to do:
Separate the halves of the peg and
glue them together back-to-back

Make a slit in the cork and push
the pointed ends of the peg into it

Stick the matches to the pegs to
make the arms

Make a cap brim from drawing
paper and stick it and the cap to
the peg

Paint the soldier

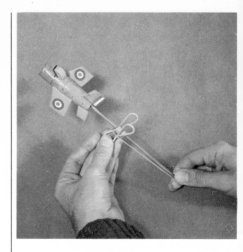

Stick the large wing to the drawing pin and the small wing to the underside of the peg

Stick the cork quarter-round to the peg to make the undercarriage

Stick the tail to the 'plane

Stick two drawing pins to the cork to make the wheels

Stick a piece of match to the nose of the 'plane to make the propeller

Paint the 'plane

Stick the 'plane to the matchbox

51 German Fighter 'Plane

You will need:

A small matchbox, a wooden peg, a used match, drawing paper, three drawing pins, a hacksaw, a quarter of a round of cork, a pin, scissors, paint, brushes

What to do:

Separate the halves of the peg

Trim one half to the shape as shown in figures A, B, C, D and E

Push a drawing pin into the top of the peg and a pin into the back underside of the peg

Cut out the shapes shown in 2

52 Delta-Wing Glider

You will need:

A large used match, stiff white paper, scissors, glue

What to do:

Cut out the wings and tail from paper

Glue them to the match, wings first and then tail

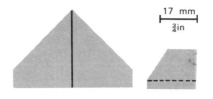

17 mm
¾in

53 Rocket-'plane

You will need:

Two corks, a half-round of cork, glue, the wire clasp from a peg, a length of slender dowelling, fine enough to pass through the spiral of the wire clasp, large elastic band, drawing paper, scissors, paint, brushes, glue

What to do:

Cut out two wings (A), two tail-planes and one tail from the drawing paper

Stick the corks together

Make slits in the corks and insert the wings and tail parts

Stick the half-round of cork to the 'plane to make the cockpit

Paint the 'plane

Push the dowelling into the back of the 'plane

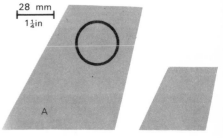

28 mm
1¼in

A

15 mm
¾in

How to launch the rocket:

Pass the elastic band round the wire clasp

Thread the dowelling through the spiral and pull the band taut

Release the band and the dowelling and the rocket will fly upwards

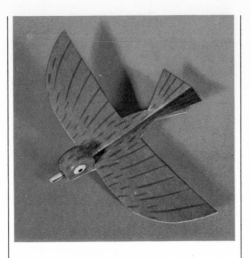

54 Mini-Glider

You will need:

Drawing paper, a small lollipop stick, a round of cork, a drawing-pin, scissors, paint, brushes, knife

What to do:

Sharpen the end of the lollipop stick and push it into the round of cork

Push the drawing-pin into the cork

Cut out the wings and the tail pieces from paper and glue them in place

Paint the glider

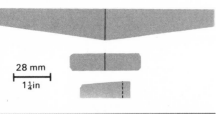

28 mm
1¼in

55 Gliding Bird

You will need:

Drawing paper, a half round of cork, two drawing-pins, a short length of matchstick, pins

What to do:

Cut out two bird shapes from paper

Glue them together along the lower halves of the body

Open the bird out and glue the cork to the front to make the head

Paint the bird

Make the eyes with drawing-pins

Push the matchstick into the head to make the beak

Balance the bird with pins stuck into the head to give extra weight

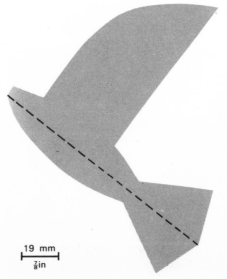

19 mm
⅞in

56 Jump Jet

You will need:

A small box of matches, drawing paper, a paper fastener, paint, brushes, scissors, glue

What to do:

Cut out the jet and its extra wing

Paint the pieces

Bend along the dotted lines

Stick the wing on

Glue A to the matchbox cover and fasten B to the drawer

Open and close the matchbox to make the jet jump

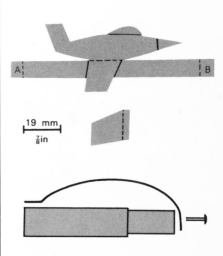

A   B

19 mm
⅞in

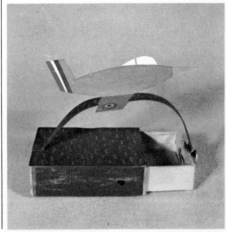

57 Little Train

You will need:

Two corks, a small eyelet hook, two open hooks, eight drawing-pins, a screw, a piece of paper, paint, scissors, brushes, pins

What to do:

Push five pins into one cork, this is the buffer

Make the chimney with the screw

Cut out the cab from paper, make a slit in the cork and insert the cab paper

Push an open hook into the back of the engine

Push drawing pins in for the wheels

Make the tender from the second cork attached to the first with the eyelet hook

58 Passenger Wagon and Truck

You will need:

Two corks, eight drawing-pins, two eyelet hooks, one open hook, four pins, a piece of drawing paper

What to do:

Cut one of the corks in half and stick four pins into the cut half, (see photograph)

Cut out the canopy shape from paper and stick it to the top of the pins. Stick four drawing-pins into the cork to make the wheels

Screw an eyelet and an open hook into the ends of the wagon

The truck is made from the other cork cut in half along two levels, the wheels and hooks are made as before

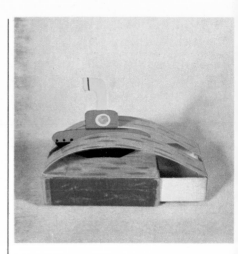

59 Midget Submarine

You will need:

Small matchbox, drawing paper, paint, scissors, glue, brushes

What to do:

Cut out the submarine and the sea from the paper

Paint them and the matchbox

Stick the submarine to the box and the sea (B) to the cover with flap C to the drawer

Open and shut the matchbox and the submarine will surface and dive

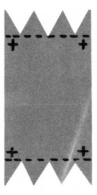

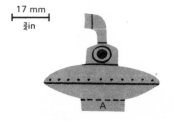

17 mm
$\frac{3}{4}$in

60 Mini-Rocket

You will need:

An aluminium cigar tube, a cork, card, glue, scissors, a length of slender dowelling which will fit through the spiral in the centre of a wire peg clasp, a wire peg clasp, a rubber band

What to do:

Cut out three fins from card

Bend them and stick them to the cigar tube

Trim a cork and push it into the open end of the tube

Push the dowelling into the cork

Paint the rocket

Fire the rocket by stretching the rubber band over the peg clasp and placing the end of the dowelling in the rubber band, stretch the band with the dowelling and release it so that the rocket flies up

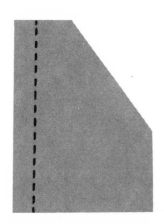

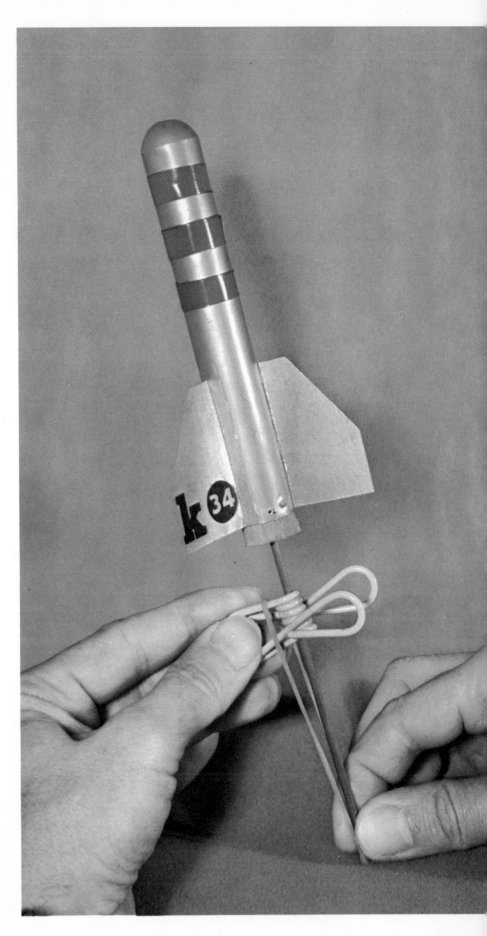

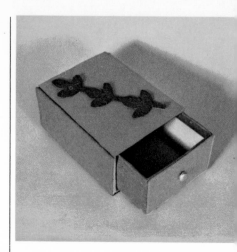

Place the round of cork in the hole so that the cork rests in the matchbox

Stick piece 3 onto the matchbox cover

Make a slit in the cork and insert the pilot

Stick the clouds to the side of the matchbox

Push the drawer of the matchbox in and out to make the pilot fly

61 Little Pilot

You will need:

A small box of matches, a round of cork, a long pin, drawing paper, scissors, glue, brushes, paint

What to do:

Cut out shapes 1, 2 and 3 from paper and paint them

Push the pin through the centre of the round of cork

Cut out a hole in the cover of the matchbox to match the hole in shape 3

62 Patience Game.

You will need:

The drawer of a small box of matches, drawing paper, paints, brushes, scissors, glue, Cellophane

What to do:

Cut a rectangle of paper to fit the matchbox drawer

Draw the head onto the paper

Cut out a pair of moustaches

Paint them

Stick the rectangle of paper into the drawer

Place the moustaches in the drawer

Cover the open side of the drawer with Cellophane

63 Little Jewel Box

You will need:

A large box of kitchen matches, green, red and blue felt, glue, a paper fastener, scissors

What to do:

Stick the felt to all sides of the matchbox (red to the top, blue to the sides, green to the front of the drawer)

Cut out the leaf pattern from green felt and stick it to the top of the box

Push the paper fastener into the drawer to make the handle

17 mm
⅔in

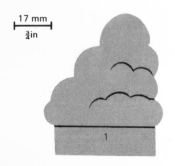

64 Mini Car

You will need:

A small box of matches, three rounds of cork, glue, paint, brushes, scissors

What to do:

The base of the car is made with the drawer of the matchbox

Stick one of the rounds of cork to the back of the drawer (spare wheel)

Cut the other two rounds of cork in half, use each half to make a wheel (the wheels are stuck to the undersides of each side of the box and the upper part of each wheel is painted in)

Cut the cover of the box into two large pieces (the sides are not used)

Fold one of the pieces into three equal parts to make the windscreen (see picture)

Cut the other piece in half and bend it into three to make the bonnet, glue in place

Paint the car

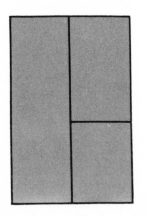

65 Fighting Cocks

You will need:

A small box of matches, drawing paper, scissors, glue, paint, brushes, paper fastener

What to do:

Cut out the shape shown below

Paint it

Bend along the dotted lines

Paint the top of the matchbox cover

Stick B to the matchbox cover

Stick A to the matchbox drawer

Push the paper fastener into the drawer

Cut the point between the beaks of the cocks

Open and shut the matchbox to make the cocks fight

B   A

18 mm
¾ in

66 Tanker

You will need:

Two small boxes of matches, a cork, a cotton reel, a small rivet, two small caps from paint tubes, glue, paint, brushes, scissors

What to do:

Cut the cork in half widthways

Cut one of the halves in half again to make two semi-circular pieces

Place one of these on one of the matchboxes to make the engine

Stick it in place with the drawer of the other matchbox stuck behind it to make the cab

Trim out the windows of the cab

Cut the remaining half cork into two rounds and cut the rounds in half and make wheels from them, (the upper parts of the wheels are painted in)

Stick the cotton reel behind the cab to make the tank

Stick the paint-tube caps to the front of the tanker to make headlights

Stick the rivet to the top of the cotton-reel tank

Paint the tanker

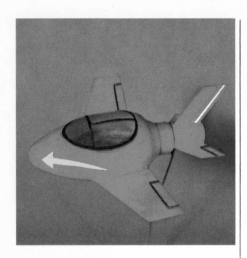

68 Sea 'Plane

You will need:

Card, scissors, paint, brushes, a half-round of cork, a nail, scissors, varnish

What to do:

Cut out either shape 1 or shape 2 from the card

Paint it

Make a slit in the flat side of the cork and insert the float of the sea 'plane

Push a nail into the rounded side of the cork

Paint and varnish the sea 'plane

Float the 'plane in a glass of water

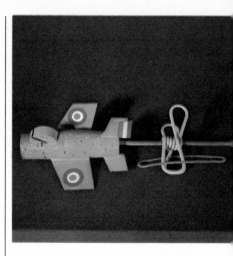

67 Fuelling 'Plane

You will need:

An old oval light bulb, Plasticine, 20cm (8in.) wire, glue, paint, brushes, scissors, drawing paper

What to do:

Wind the wire round the neck of the light bulb

Make a cork shape from the Plasticine

Push this onto the neck of the bulb

Cut out two wings, two small tailpieces and a tail fin from the paper

Stick the wings to the sides of the bulb

Stick the tailpieces and the tail fin to the Plasticine

Paint the 'plane

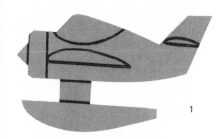

1

2

69 Catapult 'Plane

You will need:

Two corks, half a round of cork, card, the wire clasp from a peg, a length of thin dowelling, paint, brushes, scissors, glue, varnish, a rubber band

What to do:

Cut out two wings, two tail fins and a tail rudder from card

Glue the two corks together

Taper the rear cork

Cut slits in the cork and insert the wings and tail pieces

Stick the half-round of cork to the 'plane to make the cockpit

Push the dowelling into the back of the 'plane

Thread the wire clasp onto the dowelling

Fire the 'plane by slipping one end of the dowelling into one loop of the rubber band and the other loop of the band over the wire clasp

Fire the 'plane as you would fire a catapult

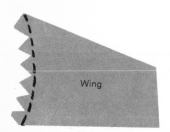

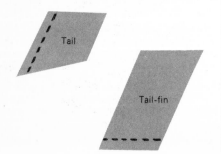

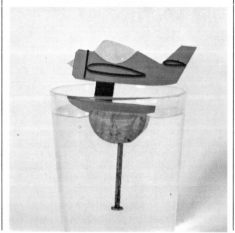

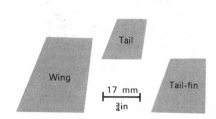

70 Closed-circuit 'Plane

You will need:

A round plaque of wood 8cm (3in.) in diameter, a cork, a large match, a tubular rivet, two safety pins, a large hairpin, drawing paper, a rubber, glue, a bodkin, thread, scissors, paint, brushes, pliers

What to do:

Cut the cork in half

Stick one half to the wooden plaque

Push the rivet into the cork

Cut the safety pins in half leaving the spiral on the pin-half

Push one into the cork to make the holding bracket and the other into the wooden plaque to make the thread guide

Make the little 'plane from the match and drawing paper with a half round of cork glued underneath the fuselage

Open out the hairpin to a right angle and push one end into the cork on the 'plane

Place the other end into the rivet after passing it through the spiral of the holding bracket

Tie the length of thread to the hairpin, thread the other end through the thread guide and tie the rubber to the free end

Wind up the thread and release the rubber, the 'plane will circle round and round

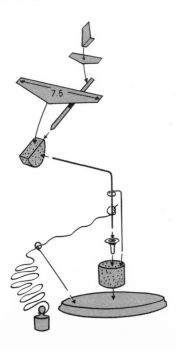

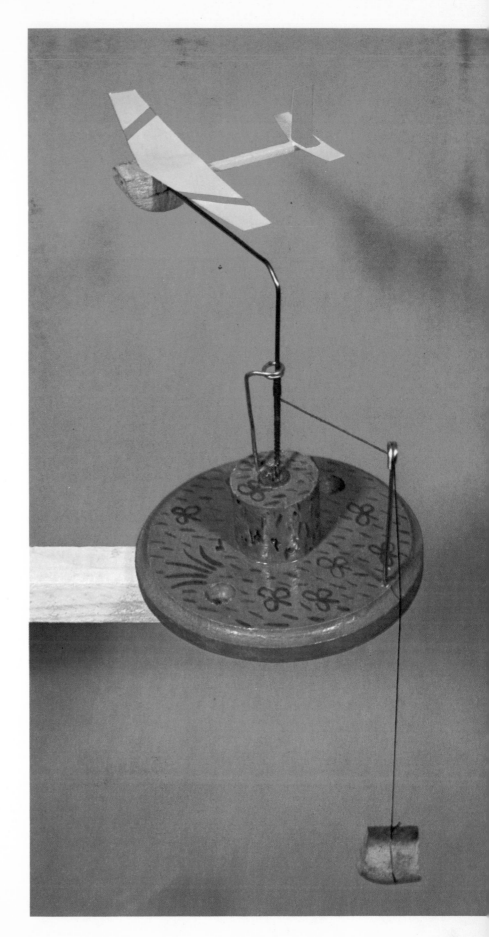

Pierce the propeller (1) with a pin and attach it to the nose of the 'plane

Stick on the wheel supports (2)

Attach the wheels to the wheel supports with a piece of the hairpin, trimmed to fit

Paint and varnish the 'plane

71 Racing 'Plane

You will need:

A wooden peg, two pins, a hairpin, two small wheels from a toy car, drawing paper, glue, scissors, paint, brushes, varnish

What to do:

Cut out the shapes below from the drawing paper

Separate the halves of the peg

Stick them together, sandwiching the wings (3) and the tail piece (5) between them

Stick on the tail piece (6) and the windscreen (4)

72 Grasshopper

You will need:

A cork, two glass headed pins (green), a matchstick, two paper-clips, glue, paint, brushes

What to do:

Push the pins into the cork to make the eyes

Cut the match in half and push each half into the cork to make the legs at the front

Glue the paper-clips to the cork to make the back legs

Paint the grasshopper

73 Yellow Snail

You will need:

A cork, cut in half lengthways, two beads, four pins, drawing paper, paint, brushes, scissors

What to do:

Taper the cork towards one end

Push a pin through each bead and then into the larger end of the cork to make the eyes

Make the horns from the other two pins

Cut out the shell shape from paper

Make a slit in the tapered end of the cork and insert the shell shape

Paint the snail

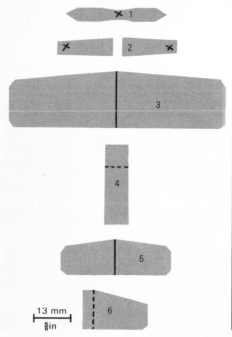

13 mm
$\frac{5}{8}$in

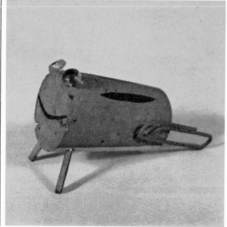

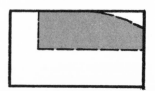

74 Jumping Frog

You will need:

Card, a round of cork cut into quarters, four little tacks, a rubber band, scissors, paint

What to do:

Cut out all the parts of the frog from card

Paint them

Cross the two longer legs and make holes on the centre where marked

Attach the crossed legs to the body of the frog where marked by pushing a tack through the body and then through the crossed legs

Hold the tack in place with a piece of cork

Attach the lower parts of the legs in the same way

Join the curved ends of the legs in the same way

Tie an elastic band between the top of the legs at the front

To make the frog jump, pull the knees apart and release them sharply

22 mm
1in

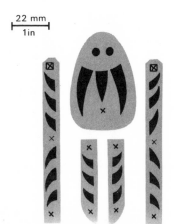

75 Basset Hound

You will need:

Two corks, six used matches, three beads, three pins, black paper, scissors, red paint, brushes

What to do:

Push four of the matches into one cork to make the legs

Attach the other cork with a match to make the head

Push a pin through each bead and then into the head to make the eyes and nose

Cut out the ears from black paper

Make slits in the head and push the ears into these

Paint the nose and the mouth

76 Little Cat

You will need:

Two corks, a knife, seven pins, three beads, drawing paper, scissors, five matches

What to do:

Push the matches into one cork to make the legs

Cut off a third of the other cork

Attach this to the body with the other match

Attach the beads to the head with pins to make the eyes and nose

Push the four remaining pins into the head to make whiskers

Cut out the ears and tail from drawing paper

Make slits in the head and body and push the ears and tail into them

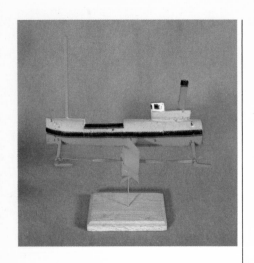

78 Small Steamboat

You will need:

A slim cotton reel, black thread, card, scissors, paint, brushes

What to do:

Cut out one shape A and two shapes B

Paint them

Paint the cotton reel

Place the boat over the reel and the two mast shapes on the boat

Pass a piece of thread from the bow of the boat, over the masts and to the stern

Glue the rigging in place

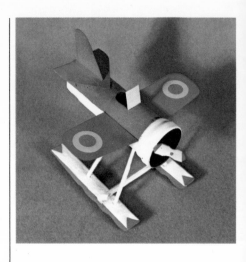

77 Turbine Boat

You will need:

Five corks, two L-shaped hooks, a straw, drawing paper, an elastic band, glue, a short length of dowelling, scissors, paint, brushes, varnish

What to do:

Cut one cork lengthwise into a third

Stick the larger part between two other corks, stick another cork on the end (hull of the boat)

Stuck the third of cork to the back of the hull to make the poop-deck

Cut the remaining cork into rounds

Cut one round into half and stick it to the poop-deck to make the control cabin

Stick the dowelling behind the cabin to make the funnel

Stick the straw to the front of the hull to make the mast

Screw the hooks into the hull at right angles

Make a turbine from a round of cork with vanes made from paper inserted into it

Thread the elastic through the turbine and hook the ends over the hooks

Paint and varnish both the boat and the turbine

Wind up the turbine, place the boat in the water and it will move

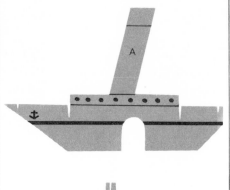

27 mm
1¼in

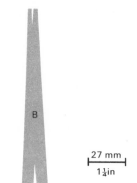

79 Red Seaplane

You will need:

Two corks, the cap of a pill tube which has the same diameter as the corks, a wooden peg, five matches, a pin, drawing paper, scissors, paint, brushes

What to do:

Stick the corks together

Stick the tube cap to the front of the corks and taper the rear cork

Cut out the propeller, the wings and the tail pieces from paper

Stick four matches into the fuselage to make the struts for the floats

Separate the peg and stick each half to the struts, stick another match between the floats

18 mm
⅞in

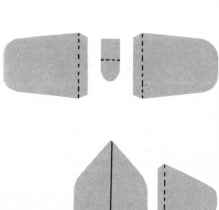

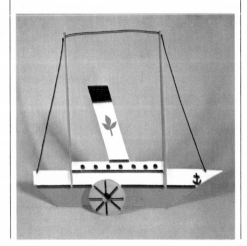

.Stick the wings and tail parts to the fuselage

Fix the propeller to the nose with a pin

Stick the windscreen to the fuselage

Paint and varnish the sea-'plane

80 Drummer Boy

You will need:

A wooden peg, two corks, two pins, a glass headed pin, two used matches, a round of cork, paint, glue, brushes

What to do:

Separate the peg and glue the pieces together back-to-back

Cut off the tip of the rounded top

Stick a cork to this

Cut one cork in half and make the drum from this

Stick the drum in place

Stick the matchstick arms to the pegs

Push the pins through the ends of the arms

Make a slot in the round of cork and push the pointed end of the drummer into it

Stick the glass headed pin into the busby

Paint the drummer

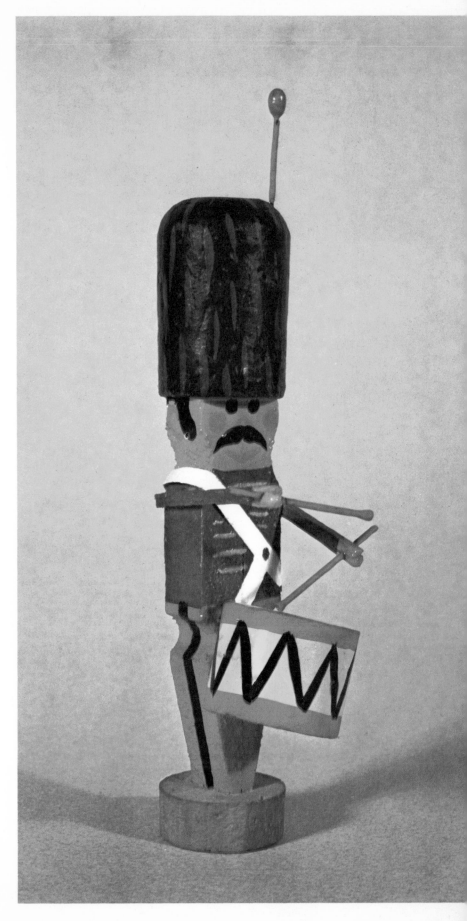

82 Blue Fish

You will need:

An egg, a matchbox, card, glue, scissors, paint, brushes

What to do:

Stick the egg to the matchbox

Cut out two fins and a tail from card

Glue them to the fishes' body

Paint the fish

81 Fighting Fish

You will need:

An egg, a rectangle of green felt 14 × 11.5cm (6½ × 6in.), a rectangle of cardboard of the same size, scraps of red felt, glue, scissors, paint, brushes

What to do:

Cut a hole in the card to fit the egg

Cut a hole in the felt to match

Cut out the fins and the tail from red felt

Place the egg in the hole and glue in place

Stick the tail and fins to the felt

Paint the fishes body

Glue the felt to the card at the edges

83 Perching Bird

You will need:

An egg, a piece of twig, two pieces of wire, each 10cm (4in.) long, a wooden base about 7cm (3in.) square, paper, card, scissors, glue, paint, brushes, wool

What to do:

Pierce two holes in the twig and two holes in the base, both at the same distance apart

Fix the wires into the twig and the base so that a perch is made

Cut out two wings, a tail, two legs and the beak from paper

Strengthen the legs by cutting card legs and sticking them to the paper legs

Stick all the pieces to the egg

Paint the bird and stick a crest of wool to its head

Make two slits in the perch and push the legs into these

13 mm
⅝in

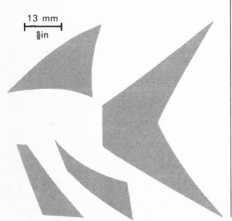

24 mm
1in

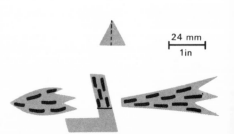

84 Chicken Egg-cosy

You will need:

Red felt, scraps of yellow, pink and black felt, pink thread and a needle, scissors

What to do:

Cut out two body shapes from red felt, two wings from pink felt, one beak from yellow felt and two eyes from black felt

Sew a wing to each body shape

Sew the eyes to the body shapes

Sew the body shapes together round the curved edges, sandwiching the beak between the shapes at the head

20 mm
7/8 in

85 Veteran Car

You will need:

A box of matches, two corks, drawing paper, scissors, paint, brushes and glue

What to do:

Cut out and fold the drawing paper according to the plan below

Stick this to the box of matches (the little line drawing shows you how to do this)

Cut one cork in two and trim one side of a half to make the engine

Stick this to the front of the car

Cut the other cork into four rounds

Stick these to the matchbox to make the wheels

Paint the car

22 mm
1 in

Folding-plan

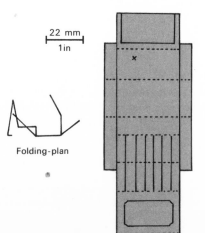

86 Another Veteran Car

You will need:

A box of matches, two corks, drawing paper, glue, scissors, paint, brushes

What to do:

Cut out and fold the drawing paper according to the plan below

Stick this to the box of matches (the little line drawing shows you how to do this)

Cut one cork in two and trim one side of this to make the engine

Cut the other cork into four rounds

Stick these to the matchbox to make the wheels

Paint the car

25 mm
1 in

Folding-plan

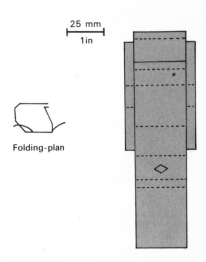

45

87 Masked Puppet

You will need:

Card, a peg, scissors, paint, brushes, a small nail, a small piece of rubber, a large hairpin

What to do:

Cut out the shape of a little man as shown in the diagram

Cut out the arm and the mask from card as shown below (correct size)

Paint both parts

Pierce the pieces at points B and C

Continue as shown in the instructions for project 30 on page 23

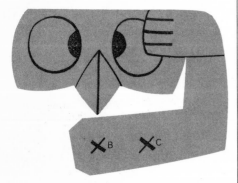

88 Drum

You will need:

A wooden cotton reel, two circles of drawing paper each measuring the same as the top of the bobbin, a length of fine wool, two matches, eight drawing-pins, glue, paint, brushes

What to do:

Stick the circles of paper to the top and bottom of the reel

Push the drawing-pins into the reel as shown in the picture

Paint the bobbin and the pins

Thread the wool in a zig-zag round the bobbin

Stick the matchsticks to the top of the drum

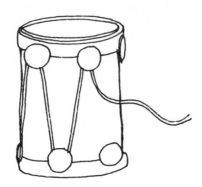

89 Little Indian

You will need:

Card, paint, brushes, scissors, a length of yellow wool

What to do:
The Horse

Cut out all the pieces and paint them

Slot them together as shown in the picture

20 mm
$\frac{7}{8}$ in

46

The Indian

Cut out all the pieces and paint them

Slot them together as shown in the picture

Make the reins with the yellow wool

90 Painted Egg

You will need:

An egg, paint, brushes, egg-cup, a bottle top

What to do:

Place the egg securely in the egg-cup

Paint the body and face of the man onto it

Stick the bottle cap on the top

91 Doll Picture

You will need:

A ping-pong ball, a cork, two used matches, beige embroidery silk, green wool, red wool, a piece of red felt 17 × 13cm (7 × 5in.) a piece of card of the same size, scissors, glue, drawing paper, paints, brushes

What to do

Stick the felt to the card

Cut the ping-pong ball in half

Cut the cork in half lengthways

Stick the half ping-pong ball to the felt to make the head

Stick the cork below it to make the body

Stick the matches to the cork to make the arms

Cut out the skirt from the pattern below, out of paper

Curve it round and stick it to the felt below the body

Make a plait 20cm (8in.) long from the beige silk

Tie each end with a green bow

Make a hanging thread from the red wool

Paint the little doll

22 mm
1 in

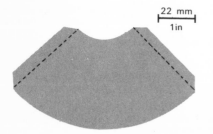

92 Little Man with a Saw

You will need:

A small matchbox, drawing paper, a small twig, a hacksaw, scissors, paint, brushes, glue

What to do:

Cut out the little man with his saw from the paper

Paint him and the matchbox top

Paint the top of the matchbox drawer

Stick the twig to the matchbox top and make a slot in it

Stick the little man to the flat side of the matchbox drawer

When the matchbox is opened and shut the man will saw the wood

16 mm
¾ in

93 Kangaroo

You will need:

A small matchbox, drawing paper, scissors, glue, paper fastener, paint, brushes

What to do:

Cut out the kangaroo from drawing paper

Paint it

Bend the base along the dotted lines

Attach A to the matchbox drawer with the paper fastener

Attach B to the matchbox cover with glue

Open and shut the matchbox and the kangaroo will bounce up and down

17 mm
¾ in

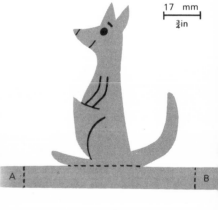

A   B

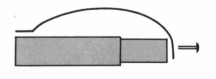

94 Nest of Birds

You will need:

A ping-pong ball, a 15cm (6in.) square of card, a square of red felt of the same size, blue and black felt, drawing paper, twigs, scissors, paint, brushes

What to do:

Stick the red felt to the card

Cut the ping-pong ball in half

Stick the halves to the felt to make the birds' heads

Cut out the branch (A, B) the birds (C and D) from felt and the beaks (E) from paper

Glue them in place

Make the nest from twigs

Paint the ping-pong balls

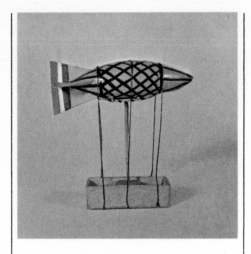

95 Airship

You will need:

A half ping-pong ball, the drawer of a small matchbox, a large hairpin, a small piece of cork, card, scissors, paint, glue, black thread

What to do:

Roll the half ping-pong ball into an oval shape

Glue it

Glue the piece of cork into the matchbox drawer

Support the airship with a hairpin pushed into the cork and into the half ping-pong ball

Cut out the tail fins and interlock them

Glue them to the half ping-pong ball

Paint the airship

Stick the threads onto the ball and round the matchbox drawer

96 Small Sailing Boat

You will need:

A cork, a large match, cotton, drawing paper, glue, scissors, paint, brushes

What to do:

Cut the cork in half lengthways

Trim it to the hull shape of the boat

Push the match into the hull

Cut out the sails and glue them to the mast

Make the rigging from cotton

Paint the boat

Varnish the hull

25 mm
1in

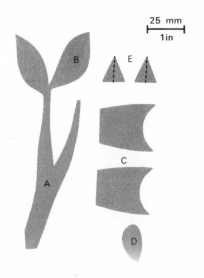

12 mm
⅝in

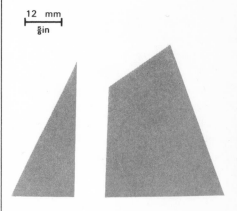

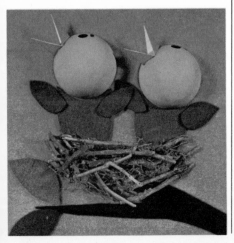

97 Little Chalet

You will need:
Two small matchboxes, card, glue, scissors, paint, brushes

What to do:
Cut out shape 1 from the card (twice)

Cut out shape 2 from card

Cut one of the matchbox covers into two pieces as shown in figure 2

Glue these pieces to the other matchbox drawer as shown

Stick shapes 1 to the ends of the chalet

Make the chimney from one of the matchbox drawers (cut and fold it to shape)

Glue the chalet to the card base

Paint the chalet

17 mm
¾ in

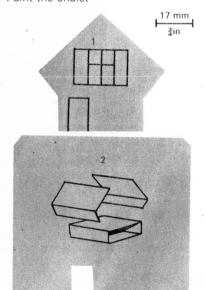

98 Rolling Dog

You will need:
A ping-pong ball, a cork, a matchstick, two hair pins, six small beads, a hook, paper, glue, black paint, a drawing-pin

What to do:
Attach the ping-pong ball to the cork with the match

Cut out the ears and glue them to the ping-pong ball

Paint them and the dog's face

Push the drawing-pin to the ball to make the nose

Thread three beads on each hairpin

Bend the hairpins into a U shape and push the ends into the cork

Push the hook into the cork

99 Pom-Pom Flower

You will need:
A half cork, a pom-pom made from sewing silk, a pin, paper, card, scissors, paint, brushes

What to do:
Stick the cork to a rectangle of card

Cut out two leaves from paper

Paint them and insert them into slits cut in the cork

Push the pin through the pom-pom and into the cork

Paint the flowerpot

100 Little Study

You will need:

Two corks, a hairpin, ten pins, a round of card 11cm (4½in.) in diameter, a round of pink felt of the same size, glue, scissors, paper

What to do:

Stick the felt to the card

Cut one cork in half lengthways

Make the table from one half

Cut the other half in half again and make the chair from these pieces

Cut the other cork into three parts and make the lamp from two of these and the hairpin

Make a tiny book from paper and stick it onto the table

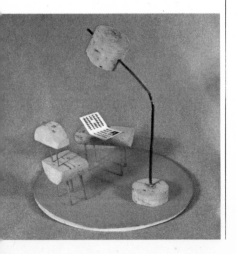

101 Old Gramophone

You will need:

A cotton reel, paper, two pins, two hairpins, a small piece of cork, drawing paper, scissors, glue, paint, brushes, felt, hack

What to do:

Cut the cotton reel in half

Glue a round of cork to the cut face

Cut the hairpin up to make the turning handle, the playing arm and the support for the sound-horn

Push these into the bobbin

Make the playing head from the little piece of cork and one pin

Attach this to the playing arm

Cut out a semi-circle of paper 3.5cm (1½in.) radius

Twist this into a cone and stick it to the support

Make a series of records from paper and place one onto the felt, held in place with a pin

Paint the gramophone

102 Guard Dog

You will need:

Two corks, a ping-pong ball, wire, a small length of chain with a clasp, paper, scissors, glue, paint, brushes

What to do:

Cut one cork in two widthways, stick one half to the other cork and round off the ends to make the dog's body

Round off one end of the half cork and stick this to the ping-pong ball to make the muzzle

Attach the head to the body with a short length of wire

Make the legs and tail from wire, and push them into the body

Cut out the ears and collar from paper

Stick them in place

Paint the dog

Attach the chain to the collar

103 Little Pump

You will need:

A ping-pong ball, a tube from a cigar, a short length of straw, a hairpin, a piece of cork which will fit into the tube, a rectangle of card, scissors, paint, brushes

What to do:

Cut off the top of the ping-pong ball, and stick the ball with the open side upwards to the card base

Push the straw into the cigar-tube as shown in the plan below

Attach the round of cork to the hairpin to make the piston as shown below, make an airhole in the cork

Pierce the cap of the tube and thread the piston handle through this

Where the ball touches the tube, make a connecting hole

Fill the ball with water, this acts as a reservoir

When the piston is raised, water will come out of the spout

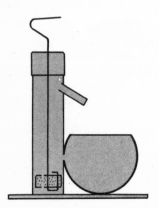

104 French Pump

You will need:

Two corks, a hairpin, a small rivet, a piece of drinking straw, a rectangle of card, glue, paint, brushes, scissors, a sharp knife

What to do:

Stick one cork upright onto a square of card

Cut a round from the other cork and stick it to the top of the first cork after trimming one side flat

Stick the piece of straw to the cork to make the spout

Stick the rivet to the top of the pump

Trim the remaining piece of cork to make a bucket shape

Use a piece of the hairpin to make the handle of the bucket

Use the rest of the hairpin to make the handle of the pump

Paint the water in the bucket and the handles

105 Windmill

You will need:

A small box of matches, a cork, two beads, a pin, card, drawing paper, greaseproof paper, scissors, paint, glue, brushes

What to do:

Cut out plan 1 from the card

Cut out plans 2 and 3 from paper

Cut out plan 4 from the grease-proof paper

Stick the drawer of the matchbox horizontally across the base of the upright cover of the matchbox

Make an air-hole connecting the drawer and the cover of the matchbox

Plan 4 is for the bellows, fold the paper along the dotted lines

The lines marked with crosses are folded inwards and the dotted lines outwards

Stick piece 1 to the top of the bellows

Place this in the matchbox drawer

18 mm
¾ in

Close the open ends of the matchbox cover with card pieces stuck in place

Make a little hole in the upper piece of card and insert the straw (This is the chimney which directs the air onto the windmill)

Cut the cork in two lengthways, stick these together and then stick them behind the matchbox cover

Make the roof with the semi-circle of paper twisted and glued into a cone

Make the windmill from piece 3 cut and folded into shape

Push the pin through this and through the two beads

Push the pin into the cork back-piece

Paint the windmill

Working the bellows will force air through the straw and cause the windmill to turn

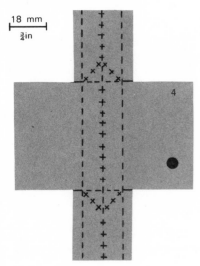

18 mm
¾in

106 Well

You will need:

A cotton reel, a round of cork, a length of wire 12cm (5in.) long or a large hairpin, cotton, a square of card 6 × 6cm (2½ × 2½in.), glue, brushes, paint, hacksaw

What to do:

Cut the bobbin in half

Stick one half to the square of card

Push the wire through the round of cork and push the ends of the wire into the bobbin

Tie the cotton to the round of cork

Paint the little well

Rest the roller on one of the matchbox drawers and stick the other drawer to the end of the first drawer

Push the two drawers in and out and the roller will roll

107 Gardener and his Roller

You will need:

Two little boxes of matches, two corks, a large hairpin, drawing paper, a bead, a pin, scissors, paint, brushes, glue

What to do:

Glue one of the corks to the cover of one of the matchboxes

Cut the other cork in two

Use one half to make the roller

Cut the other half in two again and glue one of the rounds to the upright cork to make the head

Cut out the hat from paper and push it into the round of cork after making a slot with the sharp knife

Push the pin through the bead and then into the head

Open the hairpin and thread the roller onto it, turn it on the wire until it moves freely

Bend the hairpin wire into a U shape and push the ends into the cork body of the gardener

108 Picture of Dried Leaves

You will need:

A picture from a magazine showing a country scene, a piece of card of the same size, glue, scissors, several leaves which have been pressed for at least a week in a heavy book

What to do:

Glue the picture to the card

Arrange the leaves on the picture so that they become part of the scene and give the picture more interest

Glue the leaves in place with little dabs of glue under each leaf

109 Little House

You will need:

Stiff drawing paper, glue, scissors, paint, brushes

What to do:

Cut out shapes A, B and C from the paper

Bend them along the dotted lines

Glue the walls to the base (A to C)

Glue the roof to the walls (B to A)

Paint the little house

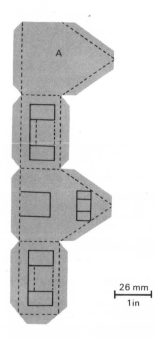

26 mm
1 in

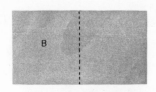

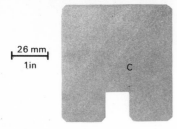

26 mm
1 in

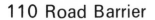

112 Tractor

You will need:

A box of matches, a cotton reel, two rounds of cork, a length of drinking straw, card, a pin, glue, scissors, paint, brushes

What to do:

Cut out shapes 1 and 2 from card, and paint them

Fold up shape 1 and glue it between the bobbin and the back of the matchbox

Glue the rounds of cork to the front of the matchbox

Push the pin through the circle (2) and into the matchbox to make the wheel

Glue the straw to the matchbox

Paint the tractor

111 Woodsman

You will need:

A small box of matches, a half cork, drawing paper, scissors, paint, brushes, glue

What to do:

Cut out the woodcutter and the ground from paper

Paint them

Glue the ground to the top of the matchbox cover

Bend the woodcutter up and glue A to the matchbox drawer

Stick the cork to the matchbox top

Make a groove in the cork so that the axe appears to chop the wood when the matchbox slides in and out

Glue the scraps of cork round the cork

110 Road Barrier

You will need:

Nine large matches, three semi-circles of cork, a rectangle of card, glue

What to do:

Push a match into each half-round of cork

Push two matches into the corks so that they are joined

Glue two matches between the uprights at the top

Glue two matches diagonally onto the upright matches

Stick the corks to the card

14 mm
⅝ in

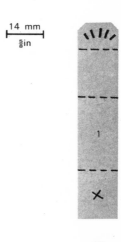

17 mm
¾ in

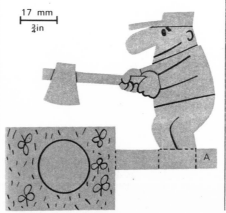

Cover the drawer of the box with green felt

Slot piece 3 into piece 1 so that piece 1 stands upright

Stick the matchbox drawer in place

Stick the canopy (2) felt to the card of the same size and stick the completed canopy in place

Stick the curtains, shutters and flowers in place

113 Window Scene

You will need:

Card, scissors, scraps of felt in blue, orange, green, black and pink, the drawer of a small box of matches, two pins, glue

What to do:

Cut out plans 1, 2 and 3 from card

Cut out plans 2, 4 (twice), 5 (twice), 6 (twice) and 7 (five times) from felt

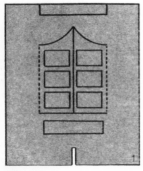

31 mm
1⅜in

31 mm
1⅜in

114 Small Cactus

You will need:

Two corks, a rectangle of card to make the base, several pins, a scrap of yellow felt, glue, scissors

What to do:

Trim one of the corks to make the pot

Cut two rounds from the other cork

Cut these rounds in half

Use three of these half-rounds to make the plant

Glue the pot to the card and the plant to the pot

Stick pins all over the cactus

Make a little yellow flower from felt

Stick a pin through it and into the cactus

Paint the cactus and pot

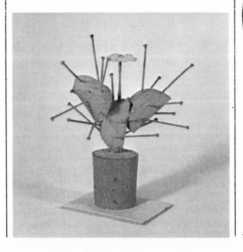

115 Mushroom Pincushion

You will need:

A cotton reel, yellow, pink and blue felt, blue embroidery silk, cotton wool, glue, scissors, pins

What to do:

Cut out two rounds of felt each of 8cm (3in.) diameter, (one pink and one yellow),

Sew diagonals of embroidery silk to the yellow felt

Stick three blue circles to the pink felt

Sew the pink and yellow felt together round the edges, inserting cotton wool as you sew

Stick the yellow felt to the bobbin

Stick pins into the mushroom

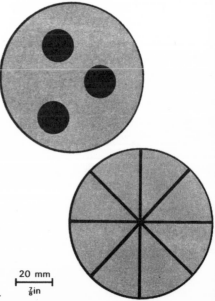

20 mm
⅞in

116 Cactus Pincushion

You will need:

A tiny plastic pot for plants, sand, plaster of Paris, green and red felt, sewing thread, cotton wool, pins, scissors

What to do:

Cut out, from green felt, three shapes A, three shapes B and six shapes C

Sew the three A shapes together to make the trunk of the cactus

As you sew, stuff it with cotton wool

Sew the shapes C together in pairs along the curved sides

Sew the shapes B into the shapes B so that they make the arms of the cactus

Stuff the arms and sew them onto the body of the cactus

Mix the sand and plaster of Paris together with a little water and fill the pot with this

Embed the cactus into this before it sets

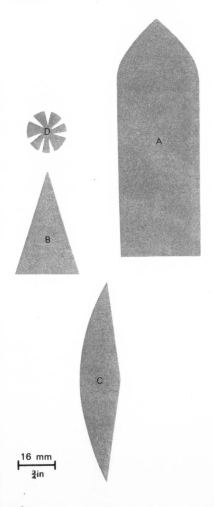

117 Wheelbarrow

You will need:

Two small rounds of cork, card, scissors, a short length of wire, glue, paint, brushes, a small drinking glass

What to do:

Cut out, from the card, two shapes A and one shape B

From shape B cut out the wheel shape (C)

Fold B along the dotted lines

Glue shapes A to shape B to make the barrow

Stick the rounds of cork to each side of the wheel

Pierce the wheel with the wire and attach the wire to each front point of the wheelbarrow

Paint the barrow

The little glass will act as a vase when placed in the hole in the barrow

118 Gardener

You will need:

The drawer from a small box of matches, four matches, a peg, two rounds of cork, a tiny bottle cap, glue, scissors, paint, brushes

What to do:

Cut off one short end of the matchbox drawer and slant the sides

Stick two matches to this end to make the wheelbarrow handles

Cut a quarter from one of the cork rounds and stick it to the wheelbarrow to make the wheel

Separate the peg and glue the halves together back-to-back to make the body of the man

Stick matchstick arms onto the body

Stick the bottle cap onto the head of the man

Push the pointed ends of the pegs into the remaining cork-round to make a base

Paint the gardener

119 Artificial Flowers

You will need:

Paper, three hairpins, three rounds of cork, a small bottle, scissors, glue, paint, brushes

What to do:

Cut out two shapes A, one shape B, one shape C and six shapes D from paper

Stick the rounds of cork into the centre of each flower (flower A has two papers, each stuck onto the cork so that the cork is hidden

Push a straightened hairpin into each cork to make a stem

Stick a pair of leaves onto each Stem

Paint the flowers and leaves

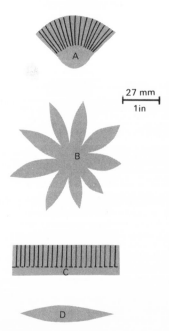

27 mm
1 in

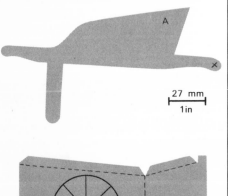

27 mm
1 in

120 Watering-can

You will need:

Two corks, a match, a hairpin, a small piece of pink felt, two pieces of green felt, scissors, paint, brushes, a pin

What to do:

Cut off a round of cork to make the rose of the can

Attach this to the complete cork with a match pointed at each end

Make the handle from the hairpin bent into shape

Cut out a pink flower and two leaves

Attach these to the can with the pin

Paint the can

Trim the base of the can to balance it

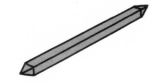

121 Garden Furniture

You will need:

Three rounds of cork, a half-cork, five matchsticks, yellow felt, scissors

What to do:

Cut two matches in half to make the legs of the table

Cut two more matches into three pieces each to make the legs for the stools

Push the legs into the corks to make the stools and table

Attach the remaining round of cork to the table with the remaining match

Cut out the table-canopy from felt

Stick it to the canopy support

Cover the top of the stools with felt

122 Flower Barrow

You will need:

A cork, two rounds of cork, paper, pink, orange and green felt, nine pins, paint, brushes, scissors

What to do:

Cut the cork in half lengthways

Attach the two rounds of cork to each side to make the wheels, use pins to do this

Push two pins into one end of the barrow to make handles

Push another pin under the cork to make the back support

Cut out a green rectangle of felt which fits the top of the barrow

Stick it in place

Cut out the canopy (3) from card, bend it and pin it to the barrow

Cut out the flowers and leaves and pin them to the barrow

Paint the barrow and canopy

1   2

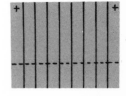

3

123 Hairdresser's Table

You will need:

A tiny pocket mirror, a half cork, a rectangle of pink felt, a scrap of red felt, braid, card, scissors, glue, paint, brushes

What to do:

Cut out plans 1, 2 and 3 in card

Cut out two shapes 4 from red felt

Fold and glue the lower table together (2)

Stick the two shapes 4 to the card front of the table-façade

Stick the mirror to the table-façade

Stick the pink felt to the top of the table

Stick two supports (3) behind the facade of the table

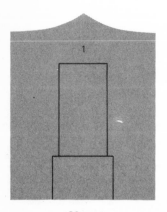

30 mm
1¼in

Stick the half-cork (seat) in front of the table

Stick a circle of red felt to the seat

Decorate the dressing table with braid

30 mm
1¼in

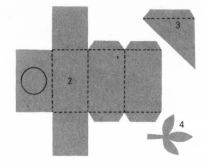

124 Doll's Lamp

You will need:

A cotton reel, drawing paper, small scraps of pink felt, glue, scissors, paint, brushes

What to do:

Using the pattern in the next column, cut out the lampshade from paper

Roll it up into a truncated cone and glue the edges together

Place this on the bobbin and glue in place

Decorate with paint and small scraps of pink felt

Make two small circles from paper strips and glue them to the sides of the lamp holder

125 Ballet Dancer

You will need:

A wooden peg, a round of cork, two used matches, blue embroidery silk, cotton wool, drawing paper, scissors, paint, brushes, glue

What to do:

Separate the halves of the peg and glue them together back-to-back

Embed the pointed ends of the peg in the round of cork

Cut out a circle of paper 9.5cm (3¾in.) in diameter

Make this into a skirt and stick it round the pegs at the waist

Tie the embroidery silk round the waist of the doll

Stick the matchsticks to the pegs to make the arms

Stick the cotton wool to the top of the pegs to make the hair

Paint the ballet dancer

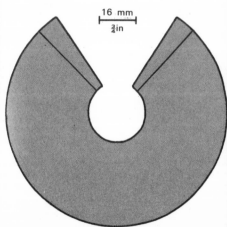

16 mm
¾in

126 Costume Doll

You will need:

Nine half walnut shells, a ping-pong ball, a round wooden or card base measuring 7cm (3in.) across pink felt, beige felt, deep pink felt, lengths of wire of 15, 10 and 7cm (6, 4 and 3in.), a fine drill, glue, scissors, paint

What to do:

Drill a hole through the curved top of five shells

Drill two holes in the pointed edges of one other shell

Stick a round of pink felt to the round of wood or card

Drill a hole in the centre of the base and insert the longest wire

Thread the five shells onto this, glueing each one in place

Thread the sixth shell onto this to make the bodice of the doll

Pierce the ping-pong ball with the end of the wire

Stick two shells to the sides of the ping-pong ball and hold them in place with the shortest wire

Stick the last shell to the top of the head

Cut out the umbrella shape (left) and the scarf (right), from felt

Push the last wire into the base

Stick the matches to the bodice to make the arms

Attach the umbrella-felt to the wire and the handle to the arm

Tie the scarf to the neck

Paint in the features

19 mm
$\frac{7}{8}$in

127 Table and Chair

You will need:

A cork, the drawer of a small box of matches, eight used matches, drawing paper, paint, brushes, glue

What to do:

Cut the cork into four rounds

Stick a round inside each end of the matchbox drawer

Push two matches into each round of cork to make the legs of the table

Turn the table right way up and cut out a cloth from drawing-paper measuring 5½ × 2cm (2 × ¾in.)

Fold the paper at each end and place it on the table

Paint the table and glue the cloth in place

Cut one of the remaining rounds of cork in two

Join the half round of cork to the remaining round with a piece of matchstick

Push three pieces of matchstick into the round of cork to make the chair legs

Paint the chair

128 Cradle

You will need:

A wooden bobbin cut in half lengthways, the drawer from a small box of matches, thin material, a large hairpin, glue, paint, brushes

What to do:

Stick the matchbox drawer to the cut side of the bobbin

Paint the cradle

Open the hairpin and bend it as shown below to make the curtain holder

Stick the hairpin to the box

Drape the material over the holder

Glue the ends to the box

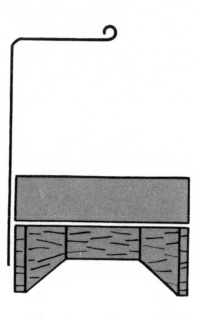

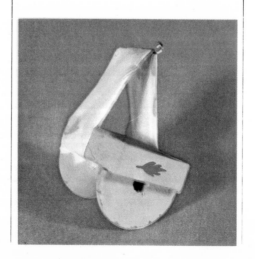

129 Chest of Drawers

You will need:

Two little boxes of matches, drawing paper, three pins, two rounds of cork, a piece of India-rubber trimmed into a cube, paint, glue, brushes

What to do:

Stick the matchboxes together

Cut one of the rounds of cork in half and use the halves to make feet for the chest

Cut out the drawing paper to make the outside of the chest (A)

Stick this round the box to hide the join

Push the pins into the drawers to make handles

Paint the chest

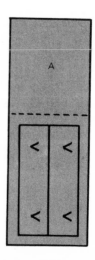

A

15 mm
¾in

The Lamp

Cut out the two shapes below from drawing paper

Stick the rubber to the circle, push the pin into the rubber and push the round of cork onto the other end

Twist the shade into a curve and stick it to the cork

Paint the lamp

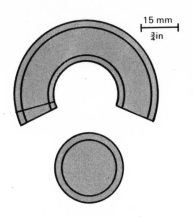

15 mm
¾in

130 Magazine Tidy

You will need:

A half-round of cork, four pins, paint, small pieces of magazines

What to do:

Push the pins into the half round of cork and paint the cork

Cut out several pieces of magazine and make them into a tiny book

Slide the book between the pins

131 Baby's Bed

You will need:

The drawer from a box of matches, a round of cork, six used matches, drawing paper, brushes, paint, glue

What to do:

Cut the round of cork in half

Stick each half to the ends of the matchbox drawer and push the matchsticks into them to make the legs

Stick the remaining matches across the top and bottom of the matchbox to support the blanket

Cut out the blanket from drawing paper (6 × 3cm (2¼ × 1¼in.))

Paint the blanket and the bed
Insert the blanket into the bed

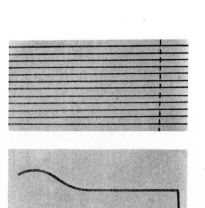

132 Rag Doll

You will need:

Two pieces of white material, cotton wool, yellow wool, needle and thread, paint, brushes, and scissors

What to do:

Cut out two shapes from the fabric as shown below

Sew them together round the edges, leaving the base open

Turn the doll inside out and fill it with cotton wool

Paint the face and hands

Close the opening at the bottom

Sew yellow wool to the head to make the hair

26 mm
1in

Stick 1 to the box to make the canopy

Stick 2 to the box to make the base of the gig

Stick the little matchbox drawer across the base of the large box to make the seat

Stick the matches to the gig to support the canopy

Stick the knitting needles to the gig to make the shafts

Open the hairpin and stick it to the front of the gig to make the whip shaft, stick the cotton to the wire to make the whip

Stick the rounds of card to the gig to make the wheels

Paint the gig

133 English Gig

You will need:

The drawer from a large box of matches, the drawer from a small box of matches, two short knitting needles, two rounds of card each 6cm (2¼in.), a large hairpin, red sewing silk, two used matches, cardboard, scissors, glue, brushes, paint

What to do:

Stand the large matchbox drawer on one end

Cut out shapes 1 and 2 from card

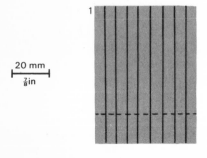

20 mm
⅞in

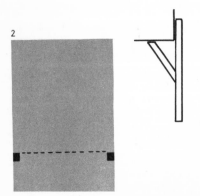

134 Four Drawers

You will need:

Four small boxes of matches, 4 paper fasteners, green felt, black and red felt, card, glue, scissors

What to do:

Stick the four boxes together (see the photograph)

Cut out a card shape to cover the top of the boxes

Stick green felt to this

Cut out a heart, spade, club and diamond from black and red felt

Glue them in place

Attach a paper fastener to each drawer to make a handle

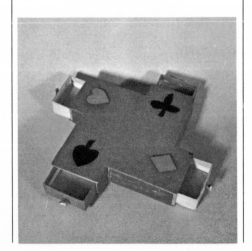

135 Farm

You will need:

The box from a 120 photographic film, card, scissors, paint, glue, brushes

What to do:

Cut out shapes A, B and C from card

Cut out shape D twice, shape E twice and shape F four times

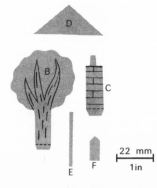

22 mm
1 in

Open out the box and make the
house and roof, insert the shapes
D to make the eaves at each end
of the house
Cut out windows and doors
Stick the tree, chimney and fence
to the house and garden
Stick the house to shape A
Paint the farm

136 Skipping Rope

You will need:
Two corks, two cotton reels,
a 60cm (24in.) length of string,
paint, glue, felt, two drawing pins,
brushes, scissors

What to do:
Glue the corks to each cotton reel
Paint the cotton reels and the
corks green
Allow the paint to dry
Stick felt over the ends of the
reels and the corks
Stick felt round the corks and
the reels
Attach each end of the string to
the corks with a drawing pin
Paint the drawing pin

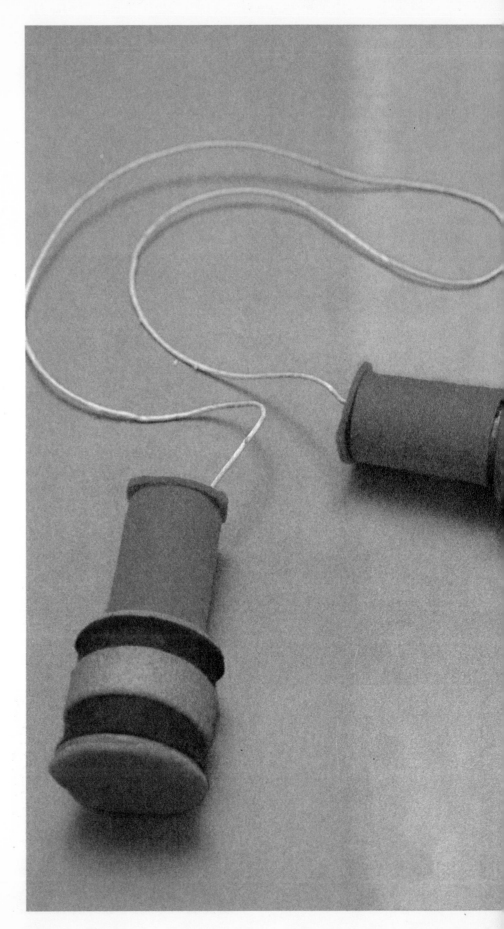

Roll the body and face of Father Christmas round a glass and glue it in place

Paint the face and cloak

Glue the beard (A) in place

Stick the frill round the face

Fill the glass with water and use Father Christmas as a vase

137 Father Christmas

You will need:
Drawing paper, glue, scissors, a cake frill, paint, brushes, a glass

What to do:
Cut out shapes A and B (shape B is shown as half of the complete shape, so cut it out double with the fold running down the face edge)

138 Lamp

You will need:
An orange, a soup-spoon of cooking oil, cotton wool, a teaspoon, a knife

What to do:
Cut the orange in half and scoop out the flesh from each half

Cut one half of the orange to make the eyes, nose and mouth of the face, cut a hole in the top of this half

Place the oil in the lower, uncut half

Make a twisted wick from the cotton wool

Place the wick in the oil and light it carefully.

Place the other half on top of the burning wick

YOU MUST ONLY LIGHT THE LAMP WHEN AN ADULT IS PRESENT

139 Christmas Salt and Pepper

You will need:
Drawing paper, card, two corks, glue, scissors, paint, brushes, salt and pepper

What to do:
Cut out two semi-circles, two beards and two circles from card (The beards can be cut from drawing paper)

Cut holes in the circles which correspond to the size of the corks

Roll the semi-circles into cones and glue them

Stick the circles to the base of the cones

Paint the cones

Stick the beards to the cones

Fill the cones with salt or pepper and make sure that the salt or pepper can escape from the top of each cone

25 mm
1 in

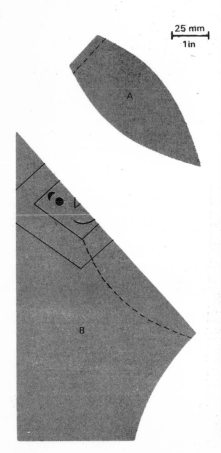

32 mm
1⅜in

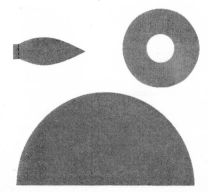

140 Christmas Tree

You will need:

A half cork, drawing paper, scissors, a length of yellow wool

What to do:

Cut out the two shapes shown below from drawing paper

Slot them together

Make a slit in the cork and insert the tree trunk

Paint the tree and the cork

Wind the wool round the tree

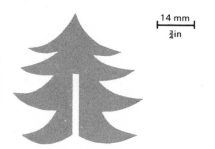

14 mm
¾ in

141 Letter Sticker

You will need:

Three rounds of stiff card each 6cm (2in.) in diameter, stuck together, a half ping-pong ball, two corks, a hairpin, paint, brushes, glue

What to do:

Stick one of the corks to the rounds of card

Stick the half ping-pong ball to the cork

Push the hairpin through the side of the ping-pong ball, through the second cork (trimmed to fit inside the ping-pong ball) and through the other side of the ping-pong ball

Paint the sticker with gloss paint

If you fill the half ping-pong ball with water and roll the flap of an envelope across the cork, the cork will rotate and wet the flap of the envelope

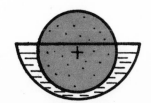

142 Calendar

You will need:

Two corks, a rectangular piece of wood, two used matches, drawing paper, scissors, paint, brushes, glue

What to do:

Cut out shape 1 from drawing paper and cut out the two openings

Roll the paper into a tube which will hold the corks and glue this tube to the wooden base

Place the two corks inside the tube and make sure that they can each turn independently

Remove the left-hand cork and draw the numbers 1 to 3 on it so that they will show in the left-hand opening of the tube

Draw the numbers 0 to 9 on the second cork so that they will show in the right-hand opening

Make 12 little month labels from card and make a holder for them by glueing the matches to the base

Paint the tube

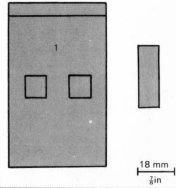

18 mm
⅞ in

67

143 Growing Snake

You will need:
A matchbox, paint, brushes

What to do:
Paint the curled body of the snake on the matchbox sleeve

Paint the curled body of the snake the snake onto the matchbox drawer

Push the drawer out slowly and watch the snake grow

144 Blue Telephone

You will need:
A cotton reel cut in half, three rounds of cork, a hairpin, a length of cotton, pliers, paint, brushes

What to do:
Cut the hairpin in half

Use one half to make the joining-part for the earphones

Cut the other half hairpin in half again and make the headrest from these

Glue a round of cork to the front of the bobbin to make the dial

Attach the earphones to the phone with the cotton

Paint the telephone

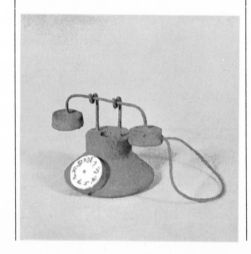

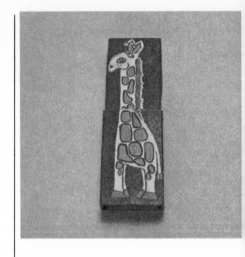

145 Growing Giraffe

You will need:
A matchbox, paint, brushes

What to do:
Draw the body of the giraffe on the matchbox cover

Draw the head and neck of the giraffe onto the matchbox drawer

Paint them

Open the matchbox and watch the giraffe grow

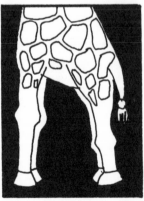

Here are some other ideas for similar toys.

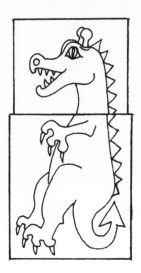

146 Egghead

You will need:

An empty eggshell, a candle, paint, a length of cotton

What to do:

Place the thread vertically in the eggshell and then fill the eggshell with melted wax

It is possible to melt the wax in a double boiler and gently heat it until it is liquid

Paint a face on the egg

CAUTION

An adult must supervise the melting and pouring of the wax

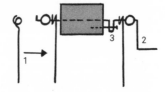

Push a pin through the U bend in the axle (3) and into the cork

Make 4 little vanes, each with a little figure of a jumping man on it

Make slots in the cork and insert the vanes

Make a small hole in the base and glue the match into this to make the checking mechanism for the little cinema

Turn the handle and watch the little man jump

147 Little Cinema

You will need:

Three rounds of thick card, each 7cm (2¾in.) in diameter, glued together, two corks, two beads, wire, a large used match, drawing paper, a pin, paint, glue, scissors, brushes

What to do:

Cut one cork in two and glue the halves to the card base

Paint the base

Push a length of wire 6cm (2¼in.) long into each half cork

Make a small ring at each end of these support wires (1)

Make an axle as shown in 2

Place a bead on the axle, pass the axle through the remaining cork, place another bead on the end and mount the axle on the support wires

148 Photograph Frame

You will need:

Two rectangles of wood, each 7 × 5cm (2¾ × 2in.), a piece of card, drawing paper, a photograph, glue, scissors, paint, brushes

What to do:

Stick the two pieces of wood together as shown in the photograph

Stick a little canopy made of card over the upper piece of wood

Stick a small label on the lower piece of wood

Stick the photograph in place

149 Magic Lantern

You will need:

Drawing paper, card, the drawer from a large box of matches, four rounds of cork, glue, scissors, paint, brushes

What to do:

Cut out from card, two of each of shapes 1, 2, 3 and 4

Cut out, once, from paper, shapes 5, 6 and 7

Assemble the first four shapes to make the body of the lantern

Stick piece 5 to the front of the lantern, bending the shape along the dotted lines

Roll piece 7 into a tube of the same diameter as piece 6, stick it along the shaded edge.

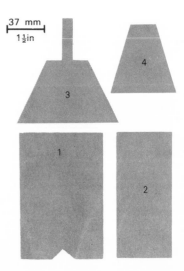

37 mm
1½in

Push the tube into the hole in
piece 5 and glue it in place

Stick piece 6 to the end of the
tube

Stick the four rounds of cork to
the base of the lantern

Paint the lantern

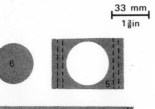

33 mm
1⅜in

150 Flowerpot

You will need:
34 large matches, yellow
embroidery silk

What to do:
Join all the matches together with
the embroidery silk, tying a knot
round each match, the matches
should be tied together at both
the top and the bottom, with the
bottom knots made more tightly
than the top ones

Place a tiny plant in a pot inside
the holder

151 Rocking Chair

You will need:
A cotton reel, cut in half lengthways, drawing paper, paint,
brushes, glue, a small hacksaw

What to do:
Cut out the shape below from
drawing paper

Make a small slit in the bobbin and
insert the shape into the bobbin

Glue it in place

Paint the bobbin and the man in
the chair

12 mm
½in

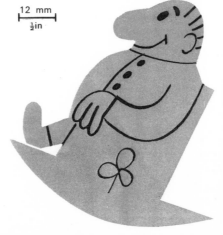

152 Television

You will need:
Two small boxes of matches, two
beads, two small pins, drawing
paper, a small photograph, glue,
scissors, paint, brushes

What to do:
Glue the two matchbox covers
together

Trim the corners of the front cover
as shown in figure 1

Cut out shape A once and shape B
twice from drawing paper

Stick these pieces to the matchbox
covers

Push the pins through the beads
and into the television to make
the tuning knobs

Paint the television

Stick the photograph into the
television screen

(The chair is the same as the one
in project 127)

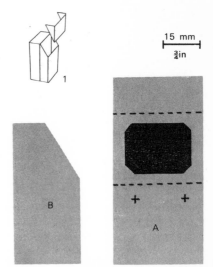

1

15 mm
¾in

B

A

Make the little delta-wing 'plane as shown in project 52

To launch the 'plane, pass the rubber band round the matchbox and drawer and pull the drawer out so that the band is stretched

Place the 'plane on the deck and release the drawer, the drawer will spring forward and push the plane off the deck.

153 Aircraft Carrier

You will need:

A small box of matches, an elastic band, a pin, drawing paper, a small used match, lightweight drawing paper, paint, glue, scissors, brushes

What to do:

Cut out shapes A and B from drawing paper

Stick shape B (folded in the centre) to the back edge of the matchbox drawer

Stick the deck (A) to the top of the matchbox cover with the rear edge sticking over the cover for 6mm ($\frac{1}{4}$in.)

Fold the control tower up at a right-angle to the deck

Paint the carrier

Push the pin through the flight deck at E, so that the pin passes through both sides of the cover and acts as a check to the drawer

154 Flag Carrier

You will need:

A peg, three used matches, the cap from a small paint tube, drawing paper, a round of cork, scissors, paint, glue, brushes

What to do:

Separate the two halves of the peg and glue them together, flat side to flat side

Push the pointed ends into the cork round and glue them in place

Stick the paint-tube cap to the top of the pegs

Stick two matches to the sides of the peg to make the arms

Make a little flag from the paper and the remaining match

Stick the flag to the right arm

Paint the flag and the flag carrier

155 Paddle Steamer

You will need:

Three corks, three large hairpins, two pins, an elastic band, drawing paper, a straw, paint, glue, varnish, scissors, brushes

What to do:

Look carefully at plans 1 and 2

The two halves of the hull are made from two corks, joined with the three hairpins, the two upper hairpins make the armature for the paddle and its elastic motor

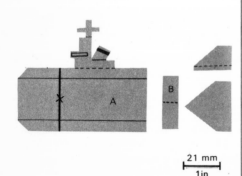

21 mm
1in

The paddle itself is made from a round of cork with eight vanes inserted into it, the elastic is threaded through the cork and attached to the hairpin armature

The rudder is made from a small rectangle of paper attached to the back of the steamer with a pin

The wheelhouse is made from a half-round of cork, stuck to the rear hull with a straw for the funnel

The whole boat is painted with enamel paint or with gouache and varnished

Wind up the elastic as shown in figure 3 and release the boat in water

156 Cork Page-Boy

You will need:
Two corks, two used matches, a bead, a pin, a nail, a felt pen, red wool

What to do:
Cut one cork in two and use one half to make the head

Cut the other half into two rounds and use one round to make the hat

Attach the hat to the head with the nail

Attach the head to the other cork with a short length of a matchstick

Push lengths of matchstick into the body to make arms

Tie red wool round the head

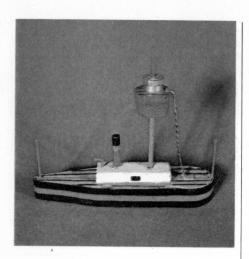

157 Marine Fire Tender

You will need:

A large wooden peg, drawing paper, two corks, the cap from a small tube of paint, four pins, a used match, a straw, scissors, paint, brushes, glue

What to do:

Separate the two halves of the peg and glue them together back to back

Cut out shapes A and B from drawing paper

Stick A round the peg

Cut out the bridge from a small piece of cork and stick it to the hull, make the funnel from a piece of straw and the ventilator from a bent pin

Stick the match to the bridge and trim the other cork to make the water holder, stick this to the match with the paint tube cap on top to make the light

Push a pin into each end of the hull and stick the ladder to the deck and the water holder

Paint the fire tender

B
A

30 mm
1¼in

158 1925 Ferry Boat

You will need:

Two large wooden pegs, a cork, a straw, a large hairpin, two pins, eight drawing pins, drawing paper, scissors, paint, glue, brushes

What to do:

Separate the pegs and glue three halves together side by side

Cut out shapes A, B and C from drawing paper and glue A and B to the sides of the hull

C is the gantry and is glued in place over the hull

Stick two pieces of hairpin to the deck to make rails for the wagon

Make the wagons from small pieces of cork with drawing pins for wheels

Stick a half round of cork to the deck to make rails for the wagons

Make the wagons from small straw, braced with a pin

The other pin is stuck into the top of the gantry

Paint the ferry boat

20 mm
⅞in

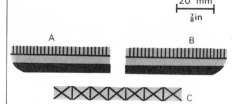

A   B

C

159 1950 Cargo Boat

You will need:

A large wooden peg, a quarter of a round of cork, a plastic straw, drawing paper, glue, paint, brushes

What to do:

Separate the halves of the peg and glue them together back to back

Cut out the sides (A) from paper and glue them round the peg

Make the wheel-house from the cork with the straw as the funnel

Paint the ferry boat

30 mm
1¼in

A

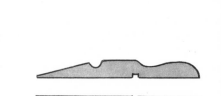

160 1960 Aircraft Carrier

You will need:

A large wooden peg, a cork, card, a plastic straw, three pins, a used match, drawing paper, paint, glue, brushes

What to do:

Open the peg and glue the halves together back to back

Glue two pieces of matchstick to the hull to make the support for the deck

Cut the deck out of card and glue it onto the supports

The bridge is made from a piece of cork cut to shape and stuck on one side of the flight deck

The funnel is a short length of plastic straw stuck behind the bridge

Glue a strip of paper round the hull and make two tiny 'planes from card, glue one to a pin and push the pin into the flight deck and the other to the deck itself

Push a pin into the top of the bridge to make a radio aerial

Paint the aircraft carrier

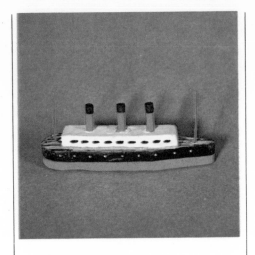

161 1930 Liner

You will need:

A large wooden peg, paper, a cork, two pins, a plastic straw, paint, glue, brushes, scissors

What to do:

Separate the halves of the peg and glue them together back to back

Cut out piece A from paper

Stick it round the peg

Make the upper cabins from a piece of cork cut from a round cork (see diagram below)

Cut three funnels from pieces of straw and glue them to the upper cabins

Push a pin into each end of the hull

Paint the liner

30 mm
1¼in

A

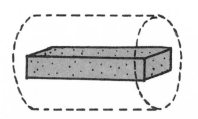

162 1950 Tanker

You will need:

A large wooden peg, a cork, a pin, a plastic straw, drawing paper, glue, paint, brushes

What to do:

Separate the halves of the peg and glue them together back to back

Cut out shape A from paper and stick it round the peg

Cut two rounds of cork, one thicker than the other, cut these rounds in half

Glue the larger half to the back part of the deck and the smaller half to the middle of the deck

Make the large funnel from the straw and the smaller funnel from a tightly rolled scrap of paper

Push the pin into the front of the deck

Paint the tanker

30 mm
1¼in

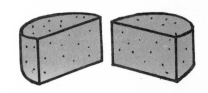

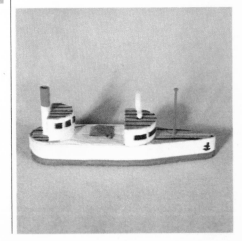

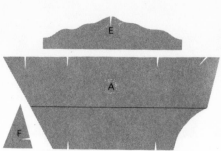

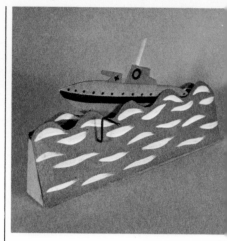

41 mm
1¾in

163 Two-Masted Yacht

You will need:

Card, scissors, paint, brushes

What to do:

Cut out shapes A, B, C and D from card

Cut out shapes E, F and G twice each from card

Paint them

Slot the shapes together as shown in the photograph

164 Wind Racer

You will need:

Two corks, two lengths of wire, each 12cm (4½in.) long, 4 beads, a rectangle of paper 6 × 9cm (2¼ × 3½in.), paint, brushes

What to do:

Cut one cork into a point at one end

Cut two rounds from the second cork

Push one of the wires through the rounds of cork and the body of the racer, enclosing the rounds with the beads, this is the axle

Bend the end of the second wire to a right-angle and push the end into the body of the racer

Make a slit in the body of the racer and insert the paper sail

Paint the sail

165 Submarine

You will need:

Card, a large hairpin, scissors, paint, brushes

What to do:

Cut out shapes A, B and C from card (cut D twice)

Pierce A and B at points D and E

Fold shape A along the dotted line and glue A and B together along the base

Insert side pieces C

Cut out the submarine (F) and pierce it at G

Paint all the pieces

Bend the hairpin as shown in diagram H

Push the pin through the side pieces and the submarine as shown in H

Turn the handle and the submarine will rise and fall

26 mm
1in

25 mm
1in

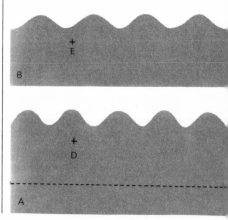

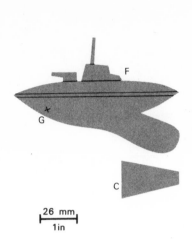

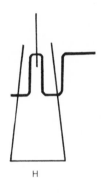

26 mm
1in

H

166 Sailor

You will need:

A used oval light bulb, small piece of modelling clay, paint, brushes

What to do:

Push the neck of the bulb into the modelling clay

Paint the bulb as shown in the picture

167 Galleon

You will need:

A wooden peg, two hairpins,
a pin, black thread, paper, paint,
glue, brushes, scissors

What to do:

Separate the halves of the peg and
glue them together back to back

Cut out shapes A, B, C and D
and G from paper

Cut out shape E four times and
shape F twice

Stick A round the peg

Stick the decks B and C to the
outer paper sides

Push the masts (made from the
hairpins) into the hull and stick
the sails (E) to them

Stick the jib boom to the front of
the hull

Stick the jib sail to the boom and
the front mast

Make the square flag from paper
(G) and the pin

Stick the pennants (F) to the
masts

Paint the galleon

Make the rigging with thread

34 mm
1⅜in

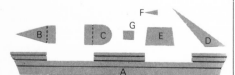

168 Three-Masted Ship

You will need:

A peg, paper, hairpins, black
thread, paint, glue, brushes

What to do:

Separate the peg and glue the
halves together back to back

Cut out all the shapes below from
paper

Wrap piece A round the pegs and
glue it in place

Make the masts from the hairpins

Stick the sails to the masts

Paint the ship

Make the rigging from thread

30 mm
1¼in

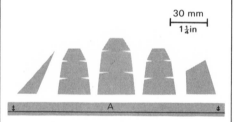

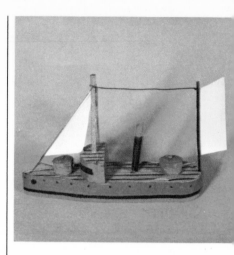

169 Steamboat

You will need:

A wooden peg, a large hairpin,
a used match, a cork, two small
paint tube caps, four pins,
a plastic straw, fuse wire, paint,
scissors, glue, brushes

What to do:

Separate the peg and glue the
halves together back to back

Cut out shapes A, B and C from
paper

Cut a round from the cork and cut
the round in half

Stick shape A round the peg,
stick the half round of cork to the
hull to make the bridge

Stick the caps to the hull to make
the guns and stick a pin to each
gun to make the gun barrels

Make the mast from the match
and the rear mast from a hairpin

Join the mast and the rear mast
with fuse wire

Make the funnel from the plastic
straw

Stick the sails in place

Paint the steamboat

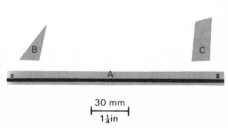

30 mm
1¼in

170 Torpedo Boat

You will need:

A peg, four used matches, a straw,
a lollipop stick, a sharp knife,
paper, glue, paint, brushes

What to do:

Separate the peg and glue the
halves together back to back

Cut out shapes A and B from
paper

Wrap shape A round the peg and
glue it in place

Fold shape B along the dotted line
and stick it to the deck to make
the front canopy

Glue the four matches to the deck
and the straw on top of these

Push the pin into the deck behind
the funnel housing

Trim the lollipop stick to two
pointed torpedo shapes and glue
these to the deck

Paint the torpedo boat

171 1830 Paddle Boat

You will need:

A peg, a cork, two caps from
small paint tubes, a hairpin,
a plastic straw, paper, scissors,
paint, glue, thread

What to do:

Separate the halves of the peg and
glue them together back to back

Cut out shape A from paper and
glue it round the peg

Trim the cork to make the wheel-
house and stick it to the deck

Make the funnel from the straw
and stick it to the wheelhouse

Stick the caps to the side of the
hull to make the paddle wheels

Make the masts from hairpin wire

Make the rigging with thread

Paint the paddle boat

172 1920 Submarine

You will need:

A peg, a hairpin, two smaller pins,
the cap from a small tube of
paint, a piece of India rubber,
drawing paper, black thread,
sharp knife

What to do:

Separate the peg and use one of
the halves

Trim the rounded end of the peg
to a point

Cut out a small circle of paper and
stick it to the peg

Stick the cap on the circle of
paper

Push a pin into the cap

Trim the rubber to make the gun
mount

Push the other pin through this
and stick the gun to the peg

Make the masts from the hairpin
and push them into the peg

Make the rigging with thread

Paint the submarine

30 mm
1¼in

A

30 mm
1¼in

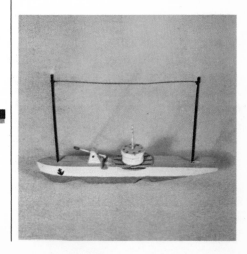

Stick the drawer of the matchbox to the hull of the boat with a bridge made from a half round of cork stuck to the prow end of the drawer

Make the chimneys from the plastic straw and stick them in place and join them with a pin

Stick the little rings to the side of the drawer

Paint the showboat

174 Growing Tree

You will need:

A matchbox, paint, brushes

What to do:

Draw and paint the trunk and lower branches of the tree on the cover of the matchbox

Draw and paint the upper branches of the tree on the matchbox drawer

Push the drawer of the matchbox out and watch the tree grow

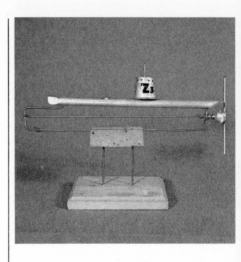

173 Show Boat

You will need:

Drawing paper, the drawer from a small box of matches, a cork, a straw, two pins, a short length of wire, two small rings, an elastic band, paint, glue, brushes

What to do:

Cut out shapes 1 and 2 from paper

Fold piece 1 and glue the prow of the boat, insert the stern piece (2) and glue it in place

Push a pin through the prow at A and B

Cut three rounds of cork, make the paddles from two of the rounds by inserting 8 little paper vanes into the rounds

Push one paddle onto the wire, push the wire through the stern and into the other paddle

Attach the elastic band to the axle and to the pin through the prow of the boat

175 Pocket Submarine

You will need:

A 13cm (5in.) length of fairly thick dowelling, a 23cm (9in.) length of wire, stiff paper, fuse wire, two small beads, a cork, an elastic band, a pin, paint, scissors, brushes, glue

What to do:

Look carefully at plans 1, 2 and 3

Cut the end of the dowelling into a V shape

Cut the other end to a slant

Bend the wire to make the shape shown in figures 1 and 3

This is the support for the elastic band and the propeller

Trim a cork to make the conning tower and glue it to a circle of paper and the dowelling

Make a propeller from a round of cork with little vanes inserted into it. Make a little hook for the propeller and place this into the propeller and also through the hook on the support, with the beads between the propeller and the support

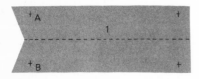

28 mm
1⅛in

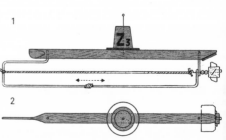

Attach the band to the propeller
hook and the other end of the
support

Paint the submarine with plastic
paint

Wind the fuse wire round the
lower part of the support to make
the submarine float low in the
water

Wind up the elastic band, place
the submarine in water and
release it

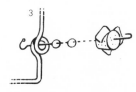

176 Saluting Sailor

You will need:
A wooden peg, a round of cork,
the cap from a small paint tube,
two matches, paint, glue, brushes

What to do:
Separate the two halves of the
peg and glue them together
back to back

Make a slot in the round of cork
and insert the pointed end of the
peg into this

Glue the cap to the top of the
peg

Glue the matches to the side of
the peg to make the arms

Paint the sailor

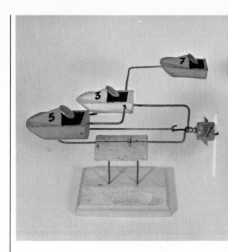

178 Tiny 'Plane

You will need:

A used match, card, glue, scissors

What to do:

Cut out the wings and the tail pieces

Glue them to the match

Launch the 'plane gently and in a slight upwards direction

177 Wolf Mask

You will need:

Card, two lengths of elastic, scissors, paint

What to do:

Cut out the mask shape

Bend along the dotted line

Make holes at A and B

Tie the elastic to the mask at A and B

Paint the mask

179 Three Speedboats

You will need:

Three corks, three drawing-pins, two lengths of wire 18cm (7in.) and 25cm (10in.), a small hairpin, two beads, an elastic band, paper, scissors, glue, paint, brushes, varnish, pliers

What to do:

Cut two corks in half and trim three of the halves to make the hulls of the boats

Cut out three triangular shapes to make the cabins and fold them down the middle

Stick them to the hulls

Push drawing-pins into the boats to make the wheels

Using the longest wire make the main armature for the propeller

Look carefully at the little diagram below which shows you how to make and attach the armature

Push the straightened hairpin through a round of cork, make a hook at one end and push the other end into the cork again

27 mm
1⅛in

12 mm
½in

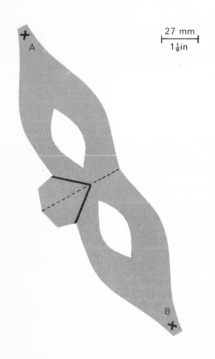

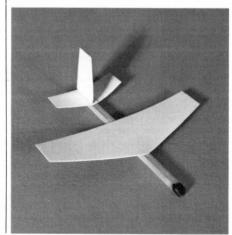

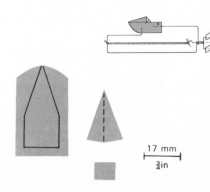

17 mm
¾in

Thread the hooked end through the little spiral on the axle, after passing it through the two beads

Make the vanes of the propeller from small squares of paper inserted into slits in the round of cork

Tie the elastic to the front of the armature and to the hook of the propeller

Cut the shorter wire in half and bend each half into an L shape

Push the end of the L into the back of the side speedboats and the other and into the sides of the centre speedboat

Paint and varnish the boats and the propeller

Place the boats in the water and wind up the propeller with a match inserted behind the propeller

Release the match and the boats will move forward

180 Tent

You will need:

A small box of matches, scissors, glue, paint, brushes, a piece of card, two matches

What to do:

Cut the cover of the matchbox into two pieces, each with a flat side and a short side

Glue them together as shown in the picture

Stick the matches to the peak of the tent at each end

Stick the lower ends of the matches to the piece of card

Paint the tent

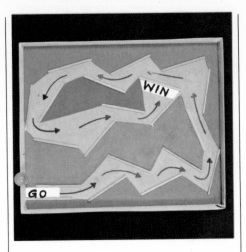

181 Marble Game

You will need:

The cover of a box 20 × 25cm (8 × 10in.), twenty used matches, a marble, glue, paint, brushes

What to do:

Draw the circuit onto the inside of the box cover

Paint it

Stick the matches onto the circuit as the picture shows

Rules

Hold the box in both hands

Place the ball at the start and try to manoeuvre the marble round the track

182 Timer

You will need:

A round of cork, a cork cut in half lengthways, a large hairpin, glue, a rectangle of card 4 × 5cm (1½ × 2in.), paint, brushes, scissors

What to do:

Trim one short edge of the card to a point

Paint a clockface on the card

Make a slit in the half cork and insert the clock face

Cut one third from the hairpin

The small part makes the hour hand

The longer part makes the minute hand

Make a hole in the centre of the clock face

Insert the hands and bend them against the face

Push the wires into the round of cork as shown in the diagram in the previous column

Set the hands to remind you of appointments

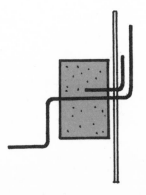

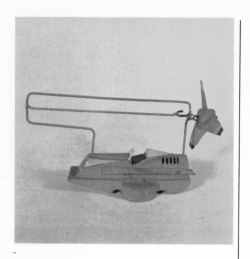

Push the small hairpin through the propeller cork and the beads and make the end into a hook

Push the hook through the spiral in the propeller support

Attach a rubber band to the propeller hook and the front of the support

Paint and varnish the boat

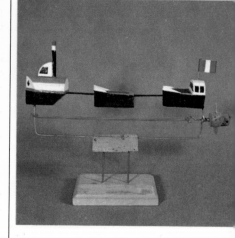

183 Boat

You will need:

Two wooden pegs, two corks, a plastic drinking straw, four pins, a small hairpin, two beads, a length of wire 25cm (10in.), paper, paint, brushes, varnish, scissors, glue, card

What to do:

Cut one cork in half lengthways

Stick the two halves end-to-end on top of three half-pegs stuck together side by side

Make the exhaust pipes at the side with plastic straws held in place with the pins

Trim the front of the cork hull to a slanted shape

Cut out and attach the wind-screen (A), the head rest (B) to the hull

Cut out three vanes (C) from card

Make a propeller from a round of cork with the vanes inserted into it

Make the stabilisers from half rounds of cork glued to the sides of the hull

Make the propeller support from the wire

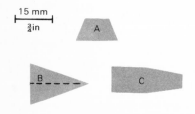

184 Binoculars

You will need:

A wooden cotton reel, a hacksaw, two corks, a short crayon, 100cm (4in.) red string, glue, two little wire rings, a stapler, paint, brushes, varnish

What to do:

Saw the cotton reel in half

Glue a cork to each half

Saw the ends off the crayon and glue it between the two halves of the binoculars

Staple the little rings to the corks on each side of the binoculars

Attach the string to the little rings

Paint the binoculars

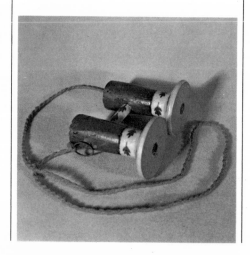

185 Whaler

You will need:

Four corks, a length of wire 38cm (15in.) long, drawing paper, two pins, an elastic band, a straw, paint, brushes, varnish, scissors, a hairpin

What to do:

Make a propeller support as shown in the photograph

Make the propeller from a half cork with paper vanes inserted into it

Attach the propeller to the support as shown in project 183

Trim one cork to make the front part of the whaler, stick a quarter cork on top to make the cabin

Stick a straw on the cork to make the funnel

Trim another half cork (cut lengthways) to make the central part of the whaler

Trim the other half to make the rear part of the whaler and stick a half round of cork onto it to make the rear cabin

Make a tiny flag from paper and make the flagpole from the pin

Push the propeller support into the front and rear part

Join the front, middle and rear part with lengths of wire cut from a hairpin

186 Buoy

You will need:

A light bulb, 50cm (20in.) wire,
card, plastic paint, brushes, a
kitchen-scale weight, scissors

What to do:

Wind the wire round the neck of
the bulb as shown in the
photograph

Make a little flag and glue it to the
top of the wire

Make a hook in the bottom of the
wire

Paint the buoy

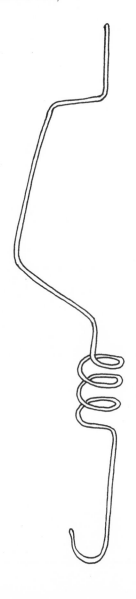

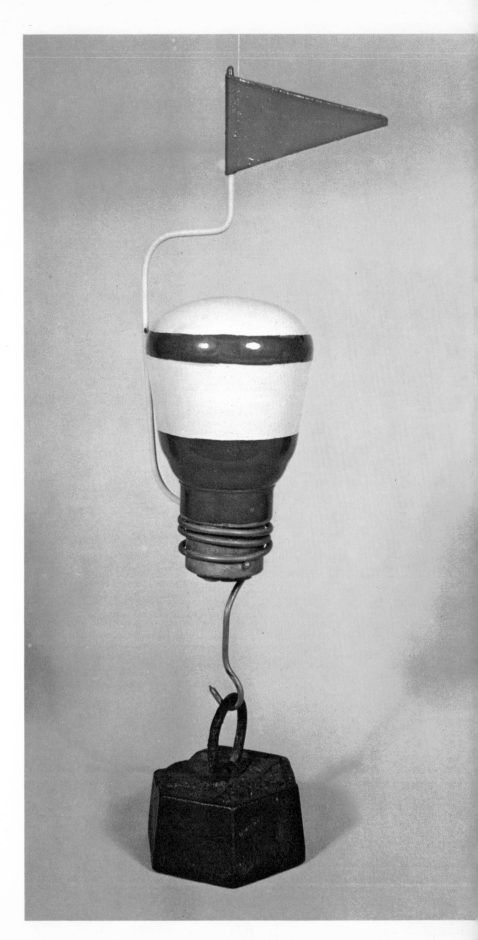

187 Grinding Mill

You will need:

Card, drawing paper, two corks, two pins, two safety pins, glue, scissors, paint, brushes

What to do:

Cut out pieces 1 and 3 from card

Cut out four pieces 2 from paper

Paint all the pieces

Cut a cork in half

Stick the halves to piece 3 to make the arch supports

Push a pin into each end of the other cork

Push the safety pins into the corks supporting the arch

Insert the vanes (2) into the cork

Place the pins in the windmill through the spirals of the safety pins

Make slits in the support corks and insert the arch

Blow on the mill and it will rotate

188 Streetlamp

You will need:

A cotton reel, a pencil, a safety pin, thread, paint, brushes, saw

What to do:

Cut the bobbin in two

Push the pencil into one half through the central hole

Cut off the fastener of the safety pin

Push one end into the top of the pencil and the other into the side of the pencil to make the bracket

Attach the other half of the bobbin to the bracket to make the lamp

Paint the streetlamp

189 Rodeo Rider

You will need:

A peg, card, sewing silk, glue, scissors, paint, brushes, saw

What to do:

Cut out shapes 1, 2 and 3 from card

Paint them

Pierce them at points A, B, C, D and E

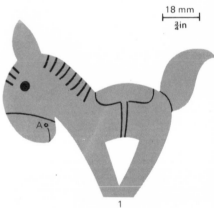

18 mm
¾ in

1

2

Bend piece 2

Cut off the rounded ends of the peg

Stick the horse's hoofs to the sawn lower edge at the front of the peg

Stick G to the back of the cowboy and to the upper part of the peg

Join E to B with black cotton

26 mm
1⅛ in

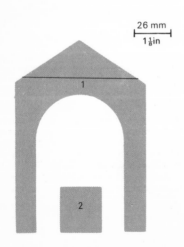

1

2

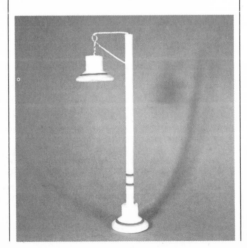

Make the bridle with embroidery silk

Open and close the peg to make the cowboy ride

18 mm
¾ in

3

190 Badminton Game (1)

You will need:

A cork, six feathers, coloured sticky tape, a bodkin, glue, a sharp knife

What to do:

Trim the base of the cork into a round shape

Make six holes in the flat end of the cork with a bodkin

Glue the feathers into the holes

Bind the cork with tape

191 Badminton Game (2)

You will need:

Two rectangles of stiff card each 22 × 16cm (9 × 6¼in.), glue, paint, brushes, scissors

What to do:

Shape the card into two bat shapes (see the picture)

Glue them together

Paint the bat

Varnish it

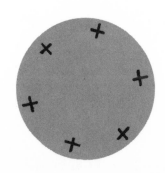

192 Hula-Hoop Game

You will need:

A small, round box lid, four rivets, a small ring, cotton, glue, paint, brushes

What to do:

Stick the rivets inside the box

Tie a knot in one end of the cotton and thread the other end through a hole in the centre of the box

Tie the other end to the ring

Paint in the numbers

Rules

Try to shake the ring onto the rivets

Have four tries and then count up your score

them to the picture

Stick little yellow scraps of felt to the picture for the grains of corn

Attach the thread to the back of the picture with the ring as a hanger

193 Chickens Picture

You will need:

Three eggs (emptied through a hole at the back), a rectangle of card 18 × 13cm (7 × 5in.), a rectangle of pink felt to match, glue, yellow, red and blue felt, a scrap of red paper, stout thread and a small ring, scissors

What to do:

Cut three holes in the card into which the eggs will fit

Stick felt over the card and cut matching holes in it

Paint the eggs and stick them into the holes

Make three little beaks from red paper and stick them to the eggs

Make five yellow wings from felt and stick them to the picture

Make 3 pairs of legs and stick them to the picture

Make the butterfly and the butterfly-net from felt and stick

194 Painted Egg (2)

You will need:

An empty egg, a length of lampshade fringe, glue, paint, coloured felt, brushes, a small cotton reel

What to do:

Glue the egg to the bobbin so that the hole through which the egg was emptied is hidden

Paint the egg

Stick the fringe round the egg to hide the bobbin

Cut out a little flower from felt and stick it to the top of the egg

195 Dancing Chicken Picture

You will need:

An empty egg, a 12cm (5in.) square of card, a square of felt to match, scraps of yellow and red felt, a scrap of red paper, glue, scissors, thread

What to do:

Cut a hole in the card into which the egg will fit

Stick the felt to the card and cut a corresponding hole

Paint the egg and glue it into the hole

Make the beak from red paper and glue it to the egg

Make the wings and feet from felt and glue them to the picture

Make a thread hanging loop

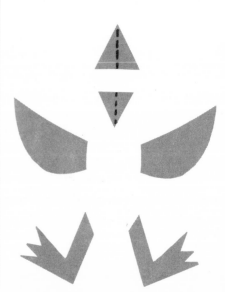

196 Hostess

You will need:

A ping-pong ball, a small cork, wire, paper, tissue paper, glue, a round wooden base, a ribbon, paint, brushes

What to do:

Look carefully at the little diagram shown below

Using the cork as a base, make legs and arms from wire

Attach the ping-pong ball to the cork with wire

Push the base of the legs into the wooden base

Cut out two of each of shapes A, B and C

Make the dress from two shapes A twisted into cones and glued to the cork (make arm holes in the cone at the top)

Wrap tissue paper round the arms, neck and legs to give them shape

Stick the side curls of hair onto the head

Paint the hostess

Tie the ribbon round the waist

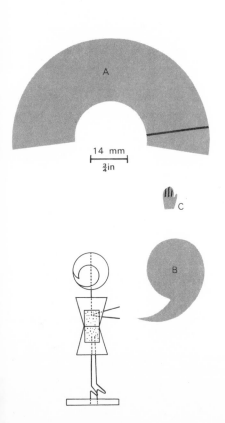

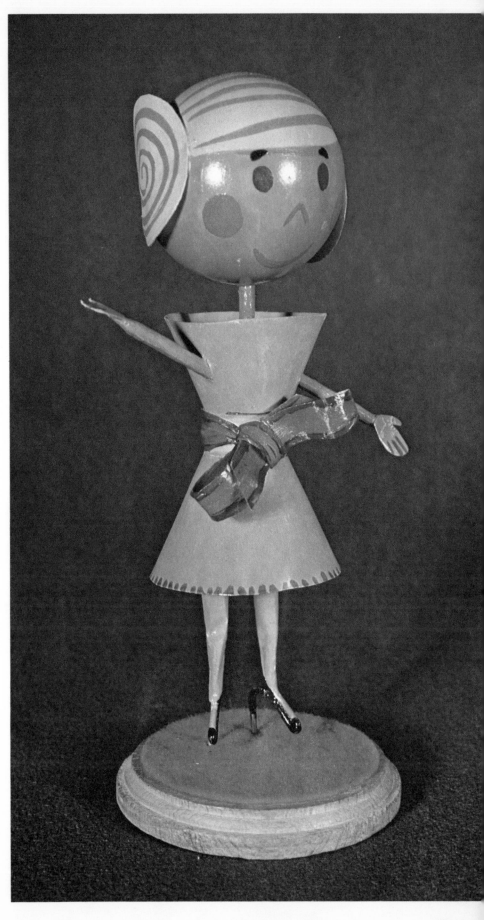

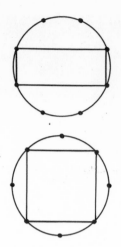

197 Rubber Band Game

You will need:
A round piece of wood about 8cm (4in.) across, eight pins, a round of paper the same size as the wood, glue, a rubber band

What to do:
Stick the paper to the wood
Push the pins in at equal spaces round the edge
Place the band round the pins

198 Patience Game, Little Car

You will need:
The drawer from a small box of matches, drawing paper, paint, brushes, two drawing pins, cellophane, glue, scissors

What to do:
Cut a rectangle of paper which will fit the inside of the drawer
Paint the car shape onto it (see the picture)
Stick the paper into the drawer
Place the two drawing pins into the drawer
Cover the open side of the drawer with cellophane
Shake the box and try to place the drawing pins where the wheels should be

199 Racket and Ball Game

You will need:
Three ping-pong balls, stiff card, three corks, strong thread, paint, glue, brushes

What to do:
Cut out the shape below from card
Stick the three corks together to make the handle of the racket
Make a slot in the top cork and push and glue the racket together
Cut two of the ping-pong balls in half
Use three of the halves to fill in the holes in the racket
Attach the thread to the ping-pong ball and to the racket
If you prefer, you can make the holes in the racket slightly smaller and not insert the half ping-pong balls
Paint the racket

Rules

Each person can move the elastic round one of the pins, the first person to make any of the three shapes shown wins

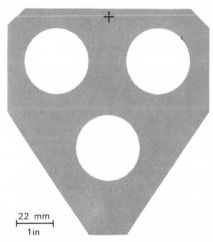

22 mm
1in

200 Yo-yo

You will need:

Four rounds of thick card, each 6cm (1½in.) in diameter, glued together in pairs, a cork, 1 metre (3 feet) of strong, smooth wool, glue, paint, brushes

What to do:

Trim the cork to a 5mm (¼in.) round and glue this between the card circles so that they are held apart

Tie the wool to the round of cork

Paint the yo-yo

Make a loop at the end of the wool for your finger

Roll the wool round and round the central spindle of the yo-yo

Put your index finger through the loop at the end of the wool and allow the yo-yo to drop towards the floor, as the yo-yo reaches the end of the wool, give the wool a sharp tug so that the yo-yo returns to your hand

201 Ball and Cone Game

You will need:

Four corks, drawing paper, coloured sticky tape, glue, scissors, compasses, paint, brushes, a ping-pong ball

What to do:

Cut out a circle from drawing paper with a diameter of 20cm (8in.)

Cut the circle in half

Make each semi-circle into a cone

Glue the corks together in pairs to make the handles

Make a triangular cut in the handles and glue the cones into these

Bind the handles with sticky tape

Paint the cones

The two players stand 5 metres apart and toss the ball from one cone to the other

202 Puppet with Hat

You will need:

A peg, drawing paper, scissors, glue, paint, brushes

What to do:

Cut out plans 1, 2 and 3 from drawing paper

Paint them

Make a slit in shape 1 at A

Pass the arm through this slit

Stick the head of the little man to the lower half of the peg

Stick the hat to the upper half of the peg

Stick the hand to the hat

Open and close the peg to make the puppet raise and lower his hat

13 mm
⅝in

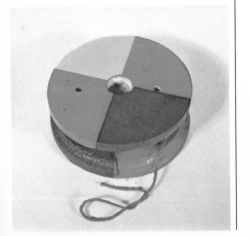

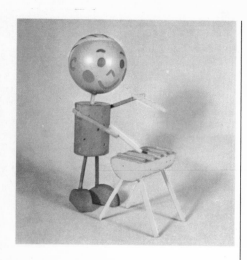

203 Musician

You will need:

A ping-pong ball, two corks, a round of cork, 14 matches, glue, paint, brushes

What to do:

Attach the ping-pong ball to the cork with a match

Cut the round of cork in two and use the halves to make the feet

Attach the feet to the body with matches

Make the arms with matches glued to the body

Make the sticks with pieces of matchstick glued to the arms

Cut the other cork in half lengthways

Push 4 matches into this to make the vibraphone

Make the keys of the vibraphone with pieces of matchstick

Paint the musician and the vibraphone

204 Drummer

You will need:

Two ping-pong balls, two corks, 11 matches, card, scissors, paint, glue, brushes

What to do:

Attach the ping-pong ball to the cork with a match

Make the arms and legs with four more matches

Cut the other cork into three rounds, cut one of the rounds in half to make the feet

Make drumsticks with pieces of matchstick stuck to the arms

Cut the other ping-pong ball in half and attach one half to a round of cork with a match

Cover the open side of the ping-pong ball with a card circle

Push three matchsticks into the remaining round of cork to make the stool

Paint the drummer, his drum and his stool

205 Little Theatre

You will need:

A small box of matches, drawing paper, a round of cork, a pin, paint, brushes, glue

What to do:

Cut out shapes A, B and C from paper

Bend B along the dotted line and stick it to the cover of the matchbox

Cut a hole in the matchbox cover to correspond with the hole in piece A

Push a pin through the round of cork and place the cork inside the matchbox

Put the cover on the box and stick A onto the cover so that the pin ends are enclosed

Make a slit in the cork round insert shape C

Paint the theatre and the puppet

Open and close the matchbox gently and the puppet will move

15 mm

¾ in

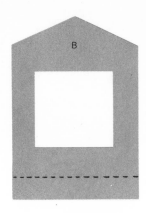

15 mm
¾in

206 Singer

You will need:

A ping-pong ball, a cork, a round
of cork, six matches, a bead,
a length of sewing silk, paint,
glue, brushes

What to do:

Attach the ping-pong ball to the
cork with a match

Cut the round of cork in two to
make the feet

Attach the feet to the cork with
matches

Bend two matches gently to make
the arms and stick these to the
cork

Make the microphone from a
match, a bead and a length of silk

Paint the singer

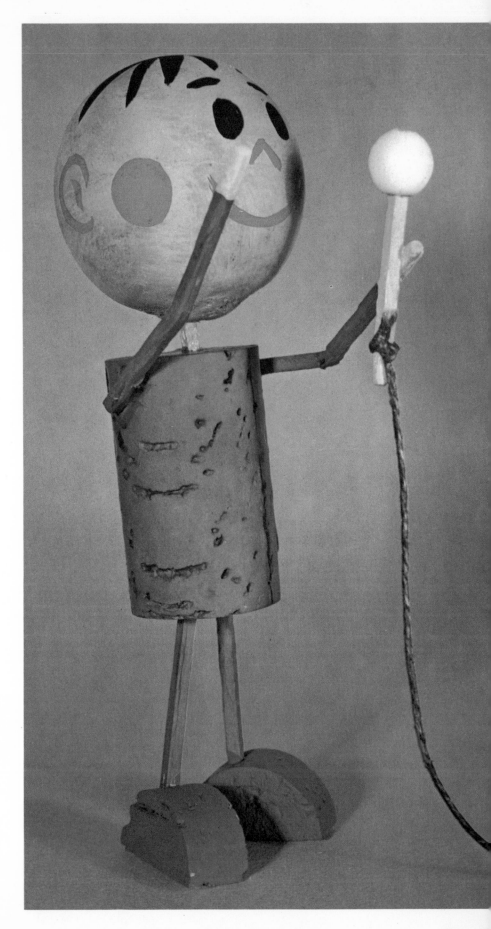

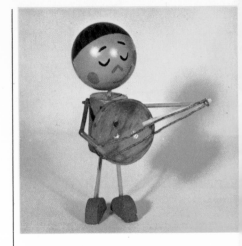

Push a ping-pong ball onto each
end of the stick

Glue the arms to the cork and to
the stick by the ping-pong balls

Paint the weightlifter

Open and close the peg and the
weightlifter will perform

207 Weightlifter

You will need:

A peg. 3 ping-pong balls, a cork,
drawing paper, a 10cm (4in.)
stick, 12cm (5in.) wire, glue,
paint, brushes

What to do:

Cut out the shape shown below
from paper (twice)

Make a hole through both halves
of the peg at the tip

Pass the wire through both holes
and wind it round the lower half
of the peg

Make a hole through the cork

Pass the wire through this hole
and through the ping-pong ball

Glue the base of the cork to the
upper half of the peg

Pierce the stick at the centre and
push the wire through this

208 Trumpeter

You will need:

A ping-pong ball, a cork, two
rounds of cork, six used matches,
glue, paint, brushes

What to do:

Attach the ping-pong ball to the
cork with a match

Cut one of the rounds of cork in
half and attach each half to the
cork with a match to make the
legs and feet

Stick two matches to the cork to
make the arms

Make the trumpet from a match
and the remaining round of cork

Stick the trumpet to the arms

Paint the trumpeter

209 Guitarist

You will need:

Two ping-pong balls, a cork,
a round of cork, six large used
matches, a length of thread, glue,
paint, brushes, a little nail

What to do:

Attach one ping-pong ball to the
cork with a match

Cut the round of cork in half and
attach each half to the cork with
a match to make the legs and
feet

Cut the other ping-pong ball in
half

Stick a match to the curved side
of the half ping-pong ball to make
the neck of the guitar

Make the string of the guitar
with thread

Glue the guitar to the body of the
little man

Stick two matches to the body to
make the arms, the right arm is
bent

Paint the guitarist

15 mm
¾in

210 Dmitri the Dancer

You will need:

A small box of matches, drawing paper, paint, brushes, scissors, glue

What to do:

Cut out the dancer from the drawing paper

Paint him

Stick A to the matchbox sleeve and B to the matchbox drawer as shown in the diagram

Open and close the matchbox to make Dmitri dance

18 mm
¾in

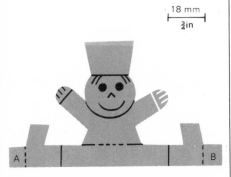

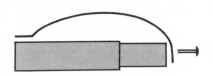

211 Ballroom Dancer

You will need:

A peg, a round of cork, two used matches, a scrap of paper, glue, paint, brushes

What to do:

Separate the halves of the peg and glue them together back to back

Make a slot in the round of cork and glue the pointed end of the peg into this

Stick a match to each side of the peg to make the arms

Cut out a dicky-front and the tails of the dress-coat from paper

Stick them to the peg

Paint the dancer

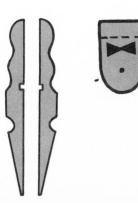

212 Musical Needles

You will need:

A wooden plaque, seven needles, fine thread, a cork, coloured sticky tape, a small hammer

What to do:

Cut the cork in half

Drill two holes in each side of the wooden base

Tie a thread into each hole, the threads should be 35cm (14in.) long

Gently hammer in seven needles into the wooden base as shown below

Decorate the corks with coloured sticky tape

One person holds the corks as if they were earphones, the other person gently plucks the needles to make them play

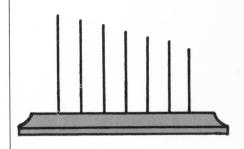

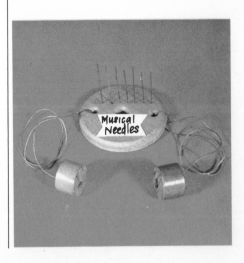

Make a little hole in the right side of the lower part of the peg

Push the right angled part of the hook into this hole

Push the hook through the hole B in the sea saw

Open and close the peg to make the see saw work

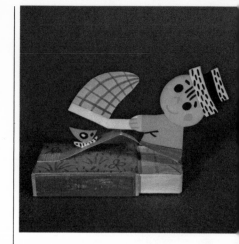

213 See Saw

You will need:

A wooden peg, a large hairpin, a small nail, a round of cork, card, scissors, glue, paint, brushes

What to do:

Cut out shapes 1 and 2 from card and paint them

Pierce them at A, B and C

Make a little hook with the hairpin as shown in figure 3

Make a slit in the upper half of the peg and insert piece 2

Push the small nail through holes C and A to join them, protect the point of the nail with a little piece of cork

214 Accordion Player

You will need:

A ping-pong ball, a cork, a round of cork, 5 used matches, a rectangle of paper 10 × 3.3cm (4 × 1¼in), paint, brushes, glue

What to do:

Attach the ping-pong ball to the cork with a match

Cut the round of cork in half and make the feet from this, attach the feet to the cork with a match for each leg

Stick a match to each side of the cork to make the arms

Paint the little man

Fold up the strip of paper into an accordion

Paint the accordion

Glue it between the arms of the little man

215 Butterfly Catcher

You will need:

A small box of matches, paper, glue, paint, brushes, scissors

What to do:

Cut out shapes 1 and 2 from paper

Paint them

Cut between the net and the strip on which the catcher sits

Stick the butterfly to the strip so that the net will cover it when the strip is flat

Bend piece 1 along the dotted lines

Glue A to the matchbox cover and B to the matchbox drawer

Open and close the matchbox to catch the butterfly

1

2

3

×
C

25 mm
1in

1

A

B

17 mm
⅝in

216 Egg Timer

You will need:

Two plastic tubes from disposable hypodermic syringes, a little very fine sand, a ping-pong ball, a cork, a round of cork, 5 used matches, a round wooden base, sticky tape, paint, glue, brushes

What to do:

Pour a little sand into each plastic tube (make a tiny paper funnel to do this)

Join the two tubes together at their open ends with sticky tape

Close the other ends with sticky tape

Make a little man as shown in project 214

Push a pin through the sticky tape which joins the two tubes so that the sand can still trickle through the tubes without being obstructed by the pin

Stick the little man to the wooden base

Paint the little man

Push the pin into the right arm of the little man so that the timer is attached to the arm

Time the sand as it trickles from one tube to the other, then work out how many times the sand-timer must be turned to give three minutes

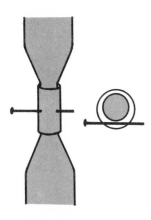

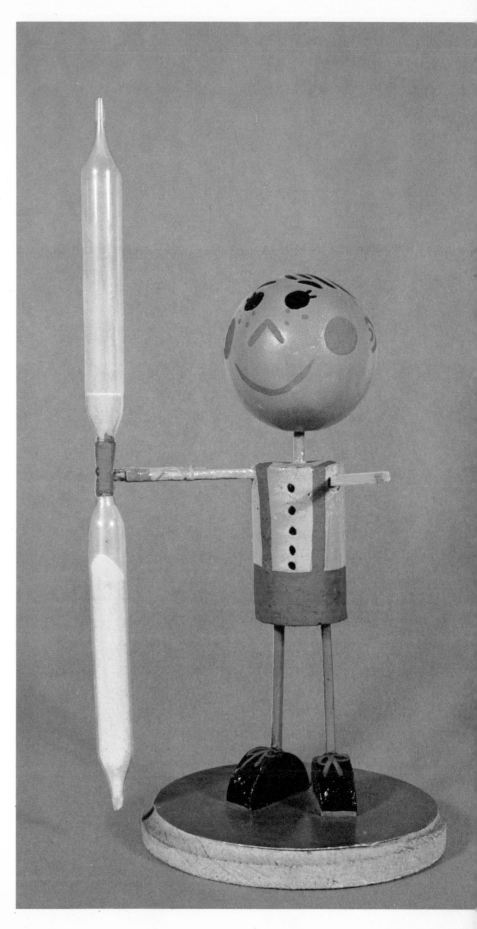

Tie the thread to point D, pass it under the peg and tie it to point F

Open and close the peg to make the sailor move the flags

217 Semaphore Sailor

You will need:

A wooden peg, card, thread, cork, two small nails, glue, paint, brushes, scissors

What to do:

Cut out the shapes below from card

Paint them

Pierce them at A, B, D, E and F

Fold flap C back and glue it to the upper part of the peg so that the little man sits astride the peg

Attach the arms at points A and E and B and G with the nails, protect the points with scraps of cork

218 Patience Game, Little Baby

You will need:

The drawer from a small box of matches, four half matches, paint, brushes, paper, glue, Cellophane

What to do:

Cut out a rectangle of paper which will fit into the drawer

Draw the baby's body and head onto the paper with dotted lines for the arms and legs

Stick the paper into the drawer

Place the four half matches in the drawer

Cover the drawer with Cellophane

219 Paper Daisy

You will need:

Card, 2 rounds of cork, scissors, glue, paint, brushes, wire

What to do:

Cut out shapes A and B from paper

Stick one round of cork to the centre of shape A and one round of cork to the centre of shape B

Stick the round of cork on the back of shape B to the centre of shape A (other side from the first round of cork)

Paint shape B yellow with black dots

Push the wire into the cork at the back of shape A

Make two leaves (C) and stick them to the wire

Paint them green

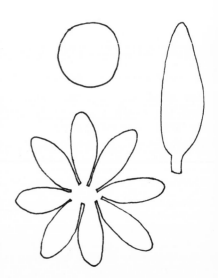

25 mm
1 in

220 Jumping Doll

You will need:

A peg, a cork, a ping-pong ball, a small ball of Plasticine, a large hairpin, a piece of paper 7 × 9cm (2½ × 3½in.) paint, brushes glue

What to do:

Drill a hole through both tips of the peg, the cork and the ping-pong ball

Pass the hairpin through all these and hook it round the lower part of the peg

Paint the little man

Fold the paper into a hat and paint it

Place the Plasticine in the hat and push the end of the wire into the Plasticine

Open and close the peg to make the little man jump

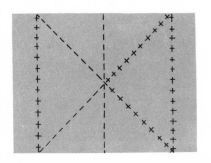

221 Balancing Act

You will need:

Card, 30cm (12in.) wire, a weight from an old pair of kitchen scales (or a set of metal washers), paint, brushes

23 mm
1 in

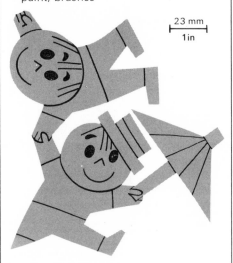

What to do:

Cut out the shape below from card

Bend the wire as shown in the photograph (the wire passes behind the little man with the umbrella to brace his legs)

Paint the shape

Glue the wire in place

Hang the weight from the end of the wire (a 200 gramme weight is ideal, but if this is unobtainable, use metal washers, adding them until the shape is balanced)

222 Telephone

You will need:

Stiff drawing paper, fine wire, two plastic bottle caps, glue, scissors, compasses

What to do:

Cut out a circle of 40cm (16in.) diameter and cut it in half

Roll each semi-circle into a cone

Glue them

Thread the wire through one of the bottle caps and knot it to keep it in place

Thread the free end of wire through one of the cones and then through the other cone and the remaining bottle cap

The wire should be at least 10 metres (12 feet) long

Two people use the telephone, each holds a cone with the wire stretched fairly tightly between the cones

One speaks and the other listens

When the telephone is not being used, wind the wire round a cork to prevent tangling

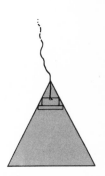

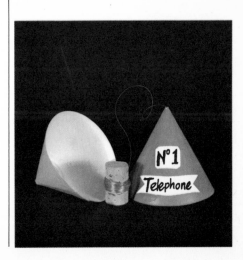

99

Stick the pill tube to the deck

Cut the cork in half and insert 8 vanes into each half

Make an axle from the wire and push it through holes A, place a bead on each end and push the paddle wheels onto the axle

Knot the elastic to the axle and to the nail at B

Paint and varnish the paddle boat

Wind up the paddles and release them when the boat is floating

224 Little Liner

You will need:

Drawing paper, paint, brushes, varnish, a half-round of cork, a nail, scissors

What to do:

Cut out the shape of the boat from the drawing paper

Paint and varnish it

Make a slit in the cork and push the base of the boat into it

Push the nail into the rounded side of the cork

Place the little boat in water, with the nail downwards

223 Paddle Boat

You will need:

Heavy card, a cork, card 11cm (8¼in.) wire, two beads, a nail, 22cm (8½in.) elastic, a small pill tube, paint, glue, brushes, a sharp knife

What to do:

Cut out shapes 1, 2 (twice) and 3 from heavy card

Cut out 16 little vanes (4) from card

Stick the hull of the boat together (pieces 1, sides 2 and deck 3)

Pierce the sides of the boat at A and the prow of the boat at B

Push the nail into B

225 Montgolfier Balloon

You will need:

A round lamp bulb, wire, a lump of Plasticine, paint, brushes

What to do:

Encircle the neck of the bulb with the wire

Make a flat loop at the free end of the wire and embed it in the lump of Plasticine

Paint the balloon

226 Unicyclist

You will need:

The cover of a small box of matches, a round of cork, small pieces of India rubber, two drawing pins, two large hairpins, 2 beads, card, scissors, paint, glue, brushes

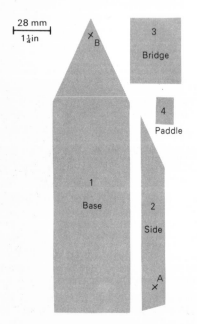

28 mm
1¼in

×B

3

Bridge

4

Paddle

1

Base

2

Side

A
×

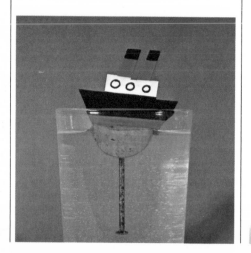

20 mm
¾in

2

3

1

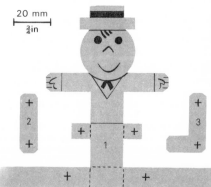

What to do:

Cut out shape 1 and shapes 2 and 3 (twice) from card

Pierce them where marked with crosses

Fold shape 1 as shown in figure 4 and stick it to the matchbox cover

Bend the hairpin as shown in figure 5

Push this through the side supports, through a bead, through the round of cork, through a bead and through the other side support (6)

Look carefully at figure 7, this shows you how to assemble the legs of the unicyclist

Paint the unicyclist

Turn the handle and watch the cyclist pedal round and round

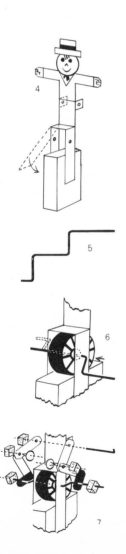

228 Gymnast

You will need:

A small matchbox, card, paint, brushes, glue

What to do:

Cut out the shape shown below from card

Paint it

Fold along the dotted lines as shown in the photograph

Glue A to the matchbox cover and C to the matchbox drawer

Open and close the matchbox to make the gymnast move

227 Fisherman

You will need:

A small box of matches, card, paint, glue, brushes

What to do:

Cut out the shape shown below from card

Paint it

Separate the head of the fish from the waves

Fold along the dotted lines

Stick A to the matchbox cover and B to the matchbox drawer

Open and close the matchbox to make the fisherman move

17 mm
¾ in

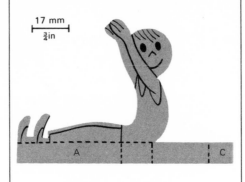

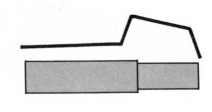

229 Little Mermaid

You will need:

A small box of matches, card, paint, brushes, glue

What to do:

Cut out both shapes shown below from card

Make the slit shown in the centre of the waves

Stick flap A to the matchbox cover

Stick flap B to the matchbox cover, pass the little mermaid through the slot and stick flap C to the matchbox drawer

Open and shut the matchbox to make the mermaid swim in and out of the waves

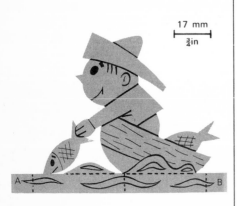

17 mm
¾ in

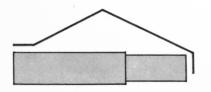

17 mm
¾ in

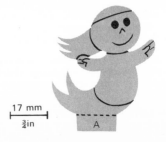

230 Acrobatic Clown

You will need:

A small matchbox, paint, brushes, scissors, drawing paper, glue

What to do:

Cut out the clown from the drawing paper

Paint him

Bend the strip along the dotted lines

Stick A to the matchbox sleeve and B to the matchbox drawer

Paint the matchbox sleeve

Move the drawer in and out to make the clown move

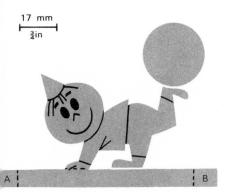

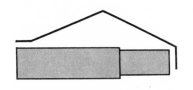

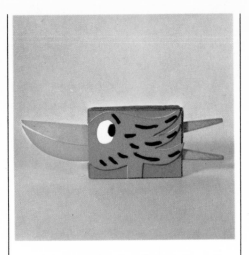

231 Talking Bird

You will need:

The cover of a box of matches, glue, drawing paper, paint, brushes, scissors, pin, small piece of cork

What to do:

Cut out pieces A and B from the drawing paper, paint them yellow

Paint the head of the bird onto the matchbox sleeve

Stick A and B to the side of the peg (see the picture)

Place the peg in the matchbox sleeve and hold it in place with a pin which passes through the matchbox and the wire spiral on the peg's spring

Protect the point of the pin with the small piece of cork

Open and close the peg to make the bird's beak move

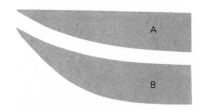

232 Lumberjacks

You will need:

A small box of matches, card, paint, glue, brushes

What to do:

Cut out shapes 1, 2 and 3 from card

Bend them along the dotted lines

Stick B to the drawer of the matchbox

Pass the trunk of the tree in front of the saw and glue the flap (C) to the matchbox cover

Stick band 2 across the band of piece A with the flaps D and E stuck to the sides of the matchbox cover

Paint all the pieces

Open and close the matchbox and the lumberjacks will saw the tree

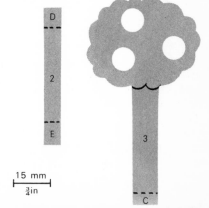

233 Little Swimmer

You will need:
A ping-pong ball, a cork, 2 rounds of cork, 5 matches, an elastic band, drawing paper, paint, glue, brushes

What to do:
Attach the ping-pong ball to the cork

Make the arms and legs with matchsticks make the feet with halfrounds of cork

Paint the swimmer

Make a propeller by inserting eight little vanes of paper into the other round of cork

Thread the elastic band through the propeller and tie the ends of the band to the arms

Place the swimmer in water and wind up the propeller, let the propeller go and the little swimmer will swim through the water

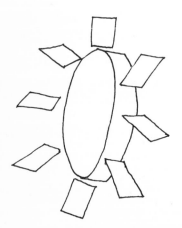

234 Fencers

You will need:
A small box of matches, paper, a paper fastener, paint, glue, paint, brushes

What to do:
Cut out the shape shown below from paper

Paint the fencers

Fold along the dotted lines

Stick A to the matchbox cover

Stick B to the matchbox drawer

Make a handle for the drawer with the paper fastener

Open and close the matchbox to make the fencers fight

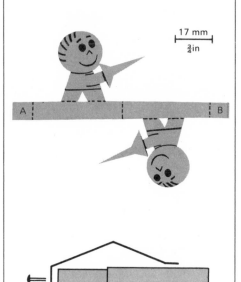

17 mm
¾in

A   B

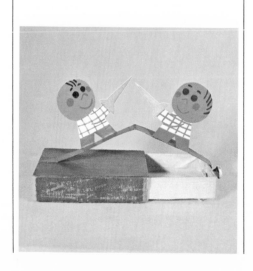

235 Sand Racer

You will need:
A cork, card, drawing paper, four lengths of wire, 9cm, 10cm, 11cm and 20cm (3½in., 4in., 4½in. and 8in.), ten beads, a length of thread, paint, glue, brushes, scissors

What to do:
Cut out a 13cm (7in.) square of paper

Roll it into a cylinder and glue the edges

Push the 10cm (4in.) wire through one end of the paper tube to make the axle of the back wheel

22 mm
1in

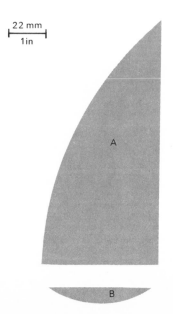

A

B

Cut the cork into three rounds, make the back wheel from one of the rounds of cork, mounted on the back axle with two beads as bearings, the axle can be seen in the photograph

Cut two rounds of card, each of a 4cm (1½in.) diameter for the wheels, stick a round of cork to each wheel

Make the front axle from the 11cm (4½in.) wire, pushed through the front of the tube, place a bead on each end of the axle and then push the wheels on to each end of the axle

Make the mast from the longest wire, pushed into the tube half way along its length, place two beads on the mast and then attach the shortest wire to the mast to make the boom

Cut out the sail (A) and tie it to the mast and glue it to the boom

Cut out the windscreen (B) and stick it to the body of the racer

Attach the boom to the body of the racer with a length of thread and a bead

236 Weightlifter (2)

You will need:
A wooden peg, three rounds of cork, three used matches, paint, brushes, glue

What to do:
Separate the halves of the peg and glue them together back to back

Make a slot in one round of cork and glue the pointed end of the peg into it

Stick two matches to the peg to make the arms

Stick the last match across these

Push a round of cork onto the ends of the crossbar-match to make the dumbells

Paint the weightlifter

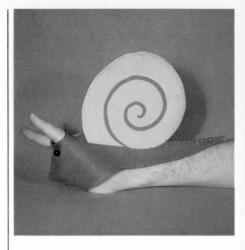

Pierce the centre of one of the card rounds and insert the sand, close the hole with sticky-tape

237 Kitchen Timer

You will need:

Two card circles, each 6cm (2½in.) in diameter, three balsa wood rods, each 9cm (3½in.), two semi circles of rigid Cellophane, each 5cm (2in.) in diameter, a band of drawing paper 1.8 × 10cm (¾ × 4in.), fine sand, glue, paint, brushes

What to do:

Roll and glue the two semi circles of Cellophane into cones

Join the two together at their points with the band of paper rolled round them

(The opening at each point must be large enough to allow the sand to fall through in a steady but fine stream)

Stick the rounds of card to each open end of the cones and support the timer with the three balsa wood strips

238 Medallion

You will need:

A ping-pong ball, two rounds of card, each with a diameter the same as that of the ping-pong ball, glue, a small photograph, red thread

What to do:

Cut the ping-pong ball in half

Stick the rounds of card to the open sides of the half ping-pong balls

Stick the photograph to one of the rounds of card

Join the two halves with red thread passing the thread through both sides of each half and leaving enough thread to knot the ends together

239 Snail Glove Puppet

You will need:

Brown felt, yellow drawing paper, two round buttons, thread, scissors, red felt pen

What to do:

Cut out two shapes A from the brown felt

Cut out shape B from the drawing paper

Join the pieces together as shown in the photograph

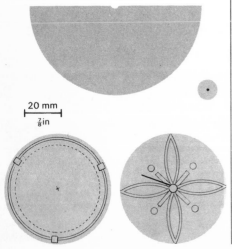

20 mm
⅞in

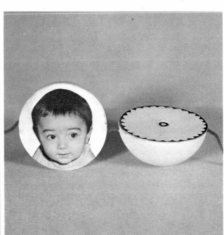

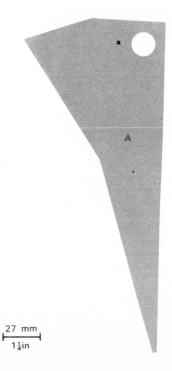

A

27 mm
1¼in

106

Sew a button to each side of the body to make the eyes

Draw a spiral on the shell with the felt pen

27 mm
1¼in

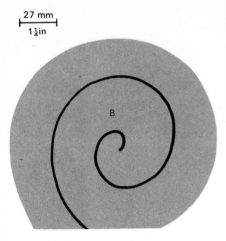

240 Flower Holder

You will need:

A half cotton reel, a rectangle of drawing paper 9 × 15cm (3½ × 6in.), glue, paint, brushes

What to do:

Roll the paper to form a cornet shape

Glue this to the bobbin

Paint and varnish it

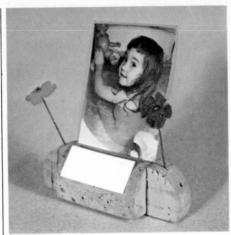

241 Small Photo-frame

You will need:

A cork, two rounds of cork, two pins, two scraps of felt, a photograph, scissors, glue

What to do:

Cut a strip lengthways from the cork so that it will stand flat

Cut the rounds of cork to make the side supports (see photograph)

Glue them to the main cork

Cut a slit in the main cork and insert the photograph

Make two tiny flowers from felt and pin them to the side corks

Make a small label from paper and stick it to the front of the main cork

242 Moving Snail

You will need:

A peg, card, scissors, glue, paint, brushes

What to do:

Cut out the shapes below from card

Paint them

Glue the shell to the lower part of the peg

Glue the head and neck to the upper part of the peg

Open and close the peg to make the snail move in and out of his shell

244 Little Imp

You will need:

A small matchbox, card, a paper fastener, glue, paint, brushes, scissors

What to do:

Cut out shapes A and B from the card and paint them

Fold A along the dotted lines and glue it to the top side of the matchbox drawer

Glue part B to the matchbox cover

Attach the paper fastener to the matchbox drawer to make a handle

Open and close the matchbox to make the imp wave his arms

243 Happy Clown

You will need:

A cotton reel cut in half, card, paint, scissors, glue, brushes

What to do:

Cut out the clown from card

Paint him

Make a slit in the bobbin and insert the clown

Paint the bobbin

245 Somersaulter

You will need:

A peg, two matches, glue, paint, brushes, a length of wire of 12cm (5in.), 2 lengths of wire of 35cm (14in.), a cork, a paint tube cap, two glue tube caps

What to do:

Open out the peg and glue the halves back to back

Glue the paint tube cap to the top of the peg

Glue the matches to the peg to make the arms

Glue the glue tube caps to the bottom of the peg to make the feet

Drill a hole through the body of the acrobat and push the shorter wire through this

Make the parallel bars from the longer wires embedded into half corks to make the bases as shown in figure 1

21 mm
1 in

11 mm
½ in

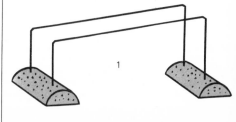

1

246 Balancing Act

You will need:

A ping-pong ball, 5 matches,
a cork, paint, glue, brushes, 15cm
(5½in.) wire, a weight from kitchen
scales or several metal washers,
a round of cork

What to do:

Push four matches into the cork
to make the arms and legs of the
acrobat

Make the feet from two half
rounds of cork

Attach the ping-pong ball head to
the cork with the remaining match

Make the wire armature as shown
in the figure below

Weight the end of the wire with
the weight from the kitchen scales
or metal washers

Paint the acrobat

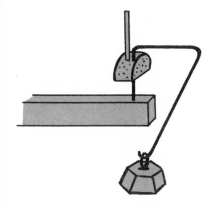

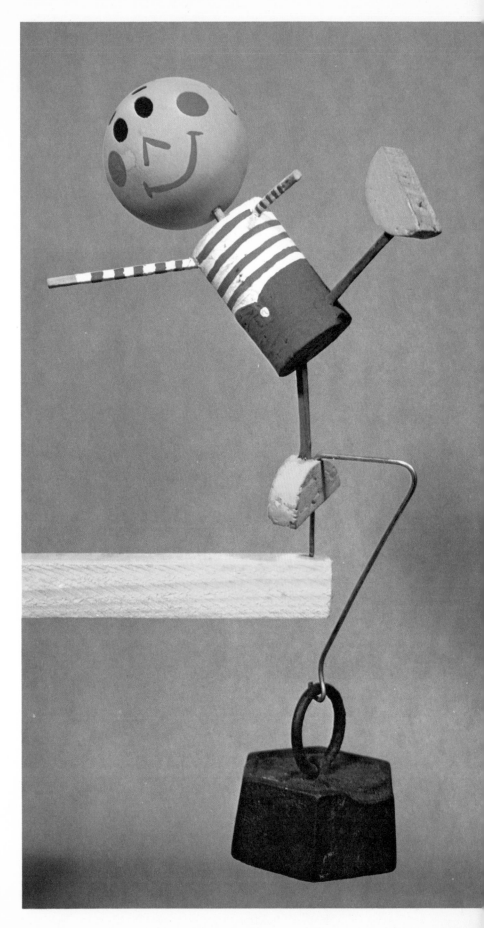

248 Little Dog

You will need:
A ping-pong ball, a cork, six matches, a length of embroidery silk, paper, glue, a black felt pen

What to do:
Make the legs and tail of the dog from matches

Attach the ping-pong ball to the body with the remaining match

Cut out two ears from paper and stick them to the head

Make the lead from silk and draw the features of the head with the black felt pen

247 Spinning Doll

You will need:
A ping-pong ball, a cork, two rounds of card stuck together each 8cm (3in.) in diameter, two matches, a length of wire 10cm (4in.) long

What to do:
Stick the cork to the rounds of card

Stick the matches to the cork to make the arms

Push the wire through the ping-pong ball, the cork and the card rounds

Paint the ping-pong ball head

Spin the doll with the tip of the wire which sticks up above the head

249 Peasant Girl

You will need:
A small, round light bulb, paper, a length of fringe, glue, paint, scissors, brushes

What to do:
Cut out the shapes shown below from paper

Roll the semi-circle round the neck of the light bulb and glue it in place

Stick the fringe to the light bulb to make the hair

Stick the basket to the front of the dress

Paint the peasant girl

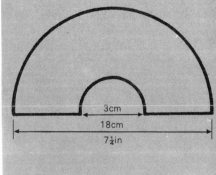

3cm

18cm

7½in

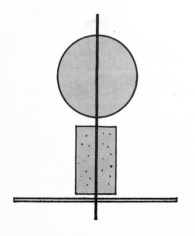

250 Baby and Cradle

You will need:
A ping-pong ball, pink felt, card, paint, glue, scissors, brushes, card

What to do:
Cut out the card shapes shown below

Stick the ping-pong ball into the hole in the card for the back of the cradle

Slot all the pieces together to make the cradle

Paint the cradle and the baby's arms

Make a little coverlet from pink felt

27 mm
1⅛in

251 Ostrich

You will need:
A cork, a half round of cork, paper, felt pens, 2 beads, two tiny nails, two matches, wire (or a hairpin)

What to do:
Cut the hairpin in two (or use the wire) and make the legs from these

Push the legs into the cork

Attach the half round of cork to the cork with a match to make the head

Push the nails through the beads and into the head to make the eyes

Cut out three shapes (below) from paper and decorate them with the felt pen

Make slits in the body and insert the paper wings and tail

252 Woodpecker

You will need:
A small matchbox, paper, scissors, glue, brushes, paint

What to do:
Cut out the shape shown below from paper

Paint it

Fold it along the dotted lines

Separate the woodpecker's chest from the tree

Glue flap A to the matchbox cover

Glue flap D to the matchbox drawer

(The little diagram below shows how the paper should be folded)

Open and shut the box and the woodpecker will peck

17 mm
⅝in

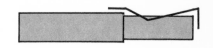

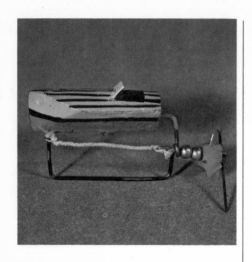

wire (see the lowest diagram, taking care to make the loop through which the propellor wire will go)

Push the ends of the base wire into the boat

Make the propellor from a small round of cork with paper vanes pushed into it

Push the straightened paperclip through the propellor and make a hook on the inner end

Slip the beads over the hook and put the hook through the loop in the base wire

Keep the paperclip in place with a small piece of rubber

Make a windscreen from paper, glued in place

Tie the rubber band to the front of the base wire and the hook of the paperclip wire

Enamel the boat and the propellor

Twist the rubber band to power the boat

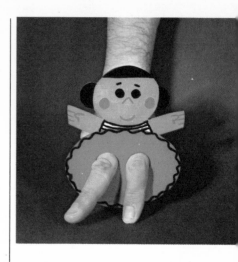

253 Little Powerboat

You will need:

A cork, a large hairpin, drawing paper, scissors, pliers, a paperclip, a small piece of India rubber, two small beads, enamel paint, brushes, a rubber band

What to do:

Cut the cork in half lengthways

Cut one of the halves in half again

Trim the quarter cork to a point at one end

Shape the hairpin into the base

254 Little Clown

You will need:

An old light bulb, shaped like a candle, the cork from a sherry bottle, string, scissors, paint, plasticine, a knife, glue

What to do:

Make a ball of Plasticine and push the neck of the light bulb into it

Paint the light bulb as shown in the picture

Cut the string into short lengths and stick it to the pointed end of the bulb to make the hair

Trim the cork and paint it

Stick it to the hair

255 Little Can-can Dancer

You will need:

Card, paint, brushes, scissors

What to do:

Draw the dancer on the card

Paint her

Cut her out

Put your index and middle finger through the holes and make her dance

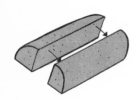

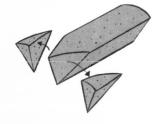

19 mm
¾in

112

256 Royal Guard

You will need:

A ping-pong ball, a cork, a sharp knife, a round of cork, a length of wire, drawing paper, 5 used matches, cotton wool, the top of a small tube of glue, glue, paint

What to do:

Cut the round of cork in half and push a match into each half to make the legs and feet

Push the matchstick legs into the cork

Push two matchsticks into the cork to make arms, bend the right arm

Make the neck from the final match

Stick the ping-pong ball to the neck

Stick the end of the glue-tube cap onto the ping-pong ball to make the nose

Stick the cotton-wool hair to the head

Cut out shapes 1 (hat), 2 (Coat-tail), 3 (cravat), 4 (coat cuffs, cut two) and 5 (spear head)

Stick them onto the guard

Paint the guard

17 mm
¾ in

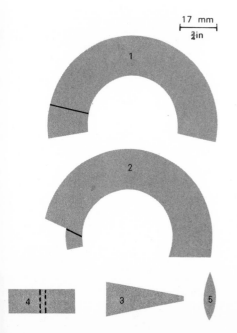

258 Grinning Mask

You will need:
Drawing paper, paint, brushes, two lengths of cork each 30cm (12in.)

What to do:
Draw the mask on the paper
Paint it
Cut it out
Make eye holes at A and B
Attach the cords at C and D

257 Moustache Mask

You will need:
Drawing paper, paint, brushes, two lengths of cord each 30cm (12in.)

What to do:
Draw the mask on the paper
Paint it
Cut it out
Make eye holes at A and B
Attach the cords at C and D

259 Frightening Mask

You will need:
Drawing paper, paint, brushes, two lengths of cord each 30cm (12in.)

What to do:
Draw the mask on the paper
Paint it
Cut it out
Make eye holes at A and B
Attach the cords at C and D

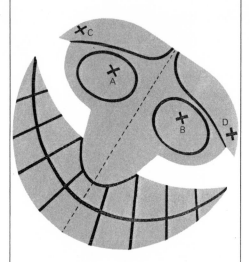

27 mm
1¼in

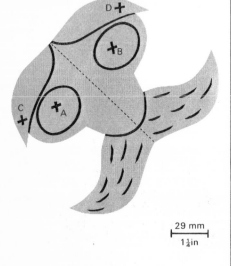

29 mm
1¼in

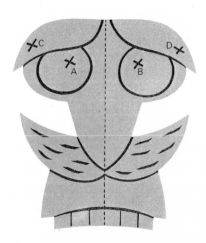

30 mm
1¼in

260 Rolling Chinaman

You will need:

Cardboard, drawing paper, scissors, paint, brushes, glue, a large marble

What to do:

Cut out a long strip (A and B) from drawing paper and two shapes C from cardboard

Paint them as shown in the diagrams

Place glue on the edges of the sides and on the flap which is shaded in the diagram

Glue the strip round the sides, but before closing the flap, insert the marble

Varnish the Chinaman

Place the Chinaman on a slope and he will roll down it

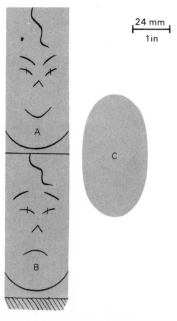

261 Cheeky Mexican

You will need:

A small matchbox, drawing paper, glue, paint, brushes, scissors

What to do:

Draw and paint A and B onto drawing paper

Stick A to the matchbox drawer

Stick B to the matchbox cover

Cut out the eyeholes on the matchbox cover

Push the matchbox drawer in and out to make the little Mexican's eyes move

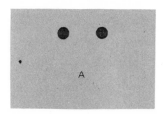

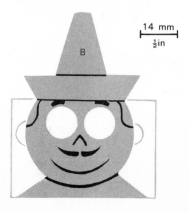

262 Cat with Moving Eyes

You will need:

A small matchbox, drawing paper, glue, paint, brushes, scissors

What to do:

Draw, paint and cut out shapes A and B onto drawing paper

Stick A to the matchbox drawer and B onto the matchbox cover

Cut out the eyeholes on the matchbox cover

Push the matchbox drawer in and out to make the cat move her eyes

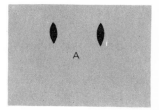

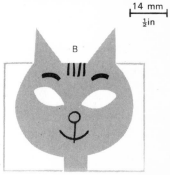

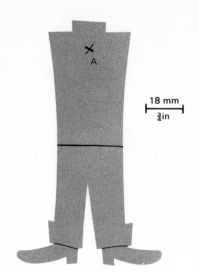

263 Happy Boy or Angry Boy?

You will need:

Card, a small nail, a scrap of cork, two lengths of thread, paint, brushes, scissors

What to do:

Cut out the shapes shown for the heads and the body of the boy

Paint them

Make holes at A, B, C and D

Join the heads to the body by pushing the small nail through holes A and B

Fold up the frowning face

Tie the threads to C and D

Hang the little boy on your bedroom door with whichever face showing so that people will know how you are feeling

264 Growing Flower

You will need:

A matchbox, paint, brushes

What to do:

Paint the stem and leaves of the flower on the cover of the matchbox

Paint the stem and the flower on the drawer of the matchbox

Open the matchbox and watch the flower grow

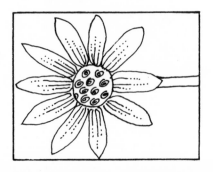

265 Three Friends

You will need:

Three light bulbs, one oval, one round and one candle shaped, card, scissors, paint, brushes, glue

What to do:

Make the card base as shown in the shape below

Paint it

Paint the bulbs as shown in the photograph

Stand the bulbs in the card base

18 mm
⅜in

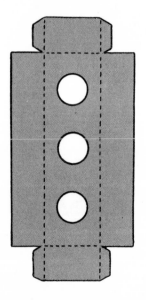

17 mm
¾in

18 mm
⅜in

116

266 Clown with Moving Eyes

You will need:

Card, paper, a small nail, two corks, a hairpin, paint, brushes

What to do:

Cut out the clown's head from card

Cut out the circle of paper and push a nail through the head at the point marked with a cross and the circle of paper where it is marked with a cross

Push the end of the nail into a half cork (see the little figure below)

Make a handle from the hairpin and push this into the half cork

Cut the remaining cork in half lengthways and make a slit in it

Push the clown's head into the slit so that it stands upright

Gently turn the handle and the clown will move his eyes

17 mm
¾ in

267 Doll Thimble-Carrier

You will need:

A cotton reel, a cork, card, red sewing silk, blue felt, glue, paint, brushes

What to do:

Stick the cork to the cotton reel

Cut out the skirt from blue felt and glue it round the cork

Make a slit in the cork and push the body and head of the doll (cut from card) into this

Paint the doll

Tie a belt of sewing silk to the doll's waist

Place the thimble on the doll's head

268 Cymbals Player

You will need:

A cork, a ping-pong ball, three rounds of cork, five matches, glue, paint, brushes

What to do:

Attach the ping-pong ball to the cork with a matchstick

Stick matchsticks to the cork to make the arms and legs

Make the feet from half rounds of cork and attach them to the legs

Stick a round of cork to each arm to make the cymbals

Paint the cymbals player

269 Doll Ring-holder

You will need:

Card, a rectangle of gingham fabric, a rectangle of card to match, four plastic cocktail sticks, a plastic bottle cap, a ping-pong ball, paper, glue, paint, brushes

What to do:

Cut out a rectangle of card 15×12cm ($6 \times 4\frac{1}{2}$in.) and cover it with gingham

Make the body of the doll from a tube of paper

Attach the cocktail sticks to make arms and legs

Stick the ping-pong ball to the body

Stick the bottle cap to the ping-pong ball

Paint the doll

Hang your rings from the doll's arms

15 mm
$\frac{5}{8}$in

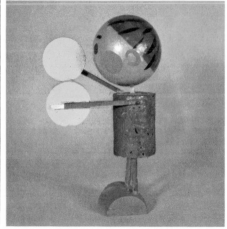

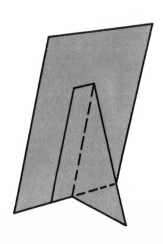

270 Scales

You will need:

A cotton reel cut in half, a crayon which will fit into the central hole of the bobbin, a large hairpin, two tiny doll's plates, a bead, red thread, glue, paint, brushes

What to do:

Push the crayon into the central hole in the bobbin

Stick the bead to the top of the crayon

Bend the hairpin as shown in the diagram below

Pass the hairpin through the bead

Attach the threads to the doll's plates to make the scale-pans

Tie the threads to each end of the hairpin

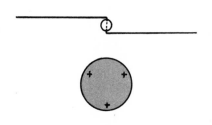

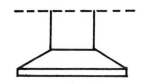

271 Pear

You will need:

A light bulb, paint, card, an elastic band, brushes

What to do:

Paint the bulb to look like a pear

Cut out the leaf shapes shown below and paint them

Attach the leaves to the neck of the bulb with the elastic band

21 mm
⅞in

272 Salt and Pepper Holder

You will need:

A ping-pong ball, a round of cork, a hairpin, four beads, two pins, paint, brushes, glue

What to do:

Cut the ping-pong ball in half and glue each half to the round of cork

(Make a slit in the cork as shown in the lower diagram)

Push the pins into the cork as shown in the upper diagram

Cut the hairpin in half and push one half into the top of the round of cork

Thread the beads onto this

Paint the ping-pong ball halves

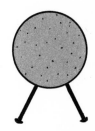

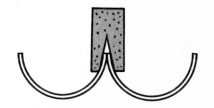

273 Ballet Dancer

You will need:
Paper, a round piece of wood 6cm
(2½in.) in diameter, a half cork,
a wire 14cm (5½in.) long, an
elastic band, paint, brushes,
scissors, glue

What to do:
Cut out the body and the legs of
the dancer from paper
Stick the half cork to the round of
wood
Stick the legs to the round of
wood
Make a slit in the cork and insert
the body of the dancer
Push the wire into the cork and
glue it to the back of the body
Paint the dancer
Make a hook in the top of the wire
and tie the elastic band to this
Tie the other end of the band to a
door handle and wind the band
up, release it and the ballet dancer
will twirl round

274 Man with Green Hair

You will need:
A small wine glass, paint, brushes,
varnish, cotton wool, grass seeds
or corn or millet or cress seeds

What to do:
Paint a face on the wine glass and
varnish it
Place the cotton wool in the glass
Sow the seeds on top and water
them a little each day
As the seeds germinate the little
man will grow green hair

275 Little Indian Girl

You will need:
A tiny bottle, a cork, two large
matches, brown wool, pink,
yellow and blue felt

What to do:
Cut the cork in half lengthways
and trim it so that it will fit into
the bottle neck
Make the hair from strands of
wool and stick them to the top of
the cork
Push the matches into the cork to
make the arms
Cut out the skirt (1) from pink felt
the belt (2) from yellow felt and
the bodice from blue felt
Cut 14 little yellow leaves for the
skirt decoration
Glue the bodice over the top of
the bottle, the skirt round the
middle of the bottle (it is easier to

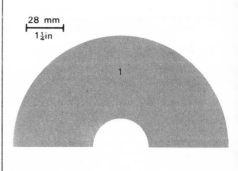

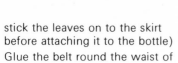

28 mm
1¼in

stick the leaves on to the skirt
before attaching it to the bottle)
Glue the belt round the waist of
the doll

276 Balancing Head

You will need:

A light bulb, wire, a weight or
several metal washers, paint,
brushes

What to do:

Paint the bulb with the features of
the head

Make an armature from the wire as
shown in the diagram below

Wind the wire round the neck of
the light bulb

Weight the end of the wire with
the weight or with several metal
washers

277 Little Tortoise

You will need:

Yellow felt, green felt, two beads, yellow sewing silk, a walnut shell, paint, varnish, glue, brushes

What to do:

Cut out the tortoise shapes from yellow and green felt

Embroider three lines on the yellow piece

Sew the pieces together round the edges

Glue the walnut shell to the green felt shape

Paint the shell

Varnish it

19 mm
¾in

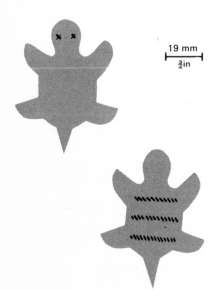

278 Diver

You will need:

Card, a cork, cut in half lengthways, a round of cork, a large hairpin, two safety pins, two nails

What to do:

Cut out the diver and the board from card

Insert this into the round of cork

Paint the diver

Push the safety pins into the half cork as shown in the photograph

Make an axle from the hairpin and attach the round of cork with the axle through the spirals of the safety pins

Push the nails into the round of cork as shown in the photograph

17 mm
¾in

279 Boy in a Swing

You will need:

A small box of matches, card, paint, scissors, brushes, glue, a length of wire 20cm (8in.) long, 2 safety pins

What to do:

Glue the two safety pins to the drawer of the matchbox as shown in the photograph

Cut out the little boy from card, paint him and glue him into the drawer

Make a swing frame from the wire and support it with the cover of the matchbox

Before you push the ends of the swing frame into the cover, thread the wire through the spirals of the safety pins

Paint the swing

280 Little Duck

You will need:

Drawing paper, a cork cut in half lengthways, a round of cork, paint, brushes, scissors, two safety pins, a screw, a hairpin

What to do:

Cut out the duck from paper and paint it

Make a slit in the round of cork and insert the duck into this

Push the safety pins into the half cork as shown in the photograph

Make an axle with the hairpin and push this through the round of cork

Support the axle with the spirals of the safety pins

Push the screw into the base of the round of cork

281 Tennis Player

You will need:

Drawing paper, a cork cut in half lengthways, a round of cork, two safety pins, a screw, a hairpin, paint, glue, brushes

What to do:

Cut out the body and arm of the tennis player from paper

Paint them

Push the safety pins into the half cork

Stick the arm of the tennis player to the round of cork

Make an axle from the hairpin and push it through the centre of the round of cork

Support the axle on the spirals of the safety pins with the body of the tennis player impaled on the end of the axle

Swing the round of cork and the tennis player's arm will move

282 Jumping Car

You will need:

A small box of matches, paper, paint, brushes, scissors, glue

What to do:

Cut out the shapes shown below from paper

Paint them

Glue the bush to the front of the matchbox cover

Fold along the dotted lines and glue flap B to the cover and flap A to the drawer

Open and close the matchbox to make the car jump

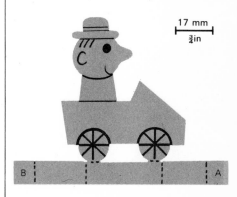

17 mm
¾ in

16 mm
⅝ in

123

283 Happy Girl or Angry Girl?

You will need:

Card, a small nail, a scrap of cork, two lengths of thread, paint, brushes, scissors

What to do:

Cut out the shapes shown for the head and body of the girl

Paint them

Make holes at A, B, C and D

Join the heads to the body with the small nail and protect the head of the nail with a scrap of cork

Fold up the frowning face

Tie the threads to C and D

Hang the little girl on your bedroom door with whichever face showing so that people will know how you are feeling

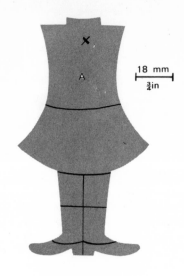

18 mm
¾in

284 Bracelet

You will need:

Six rounds of cork, eleven beads, yellow sewing silk, a needle, scissors

What to do:

Cut the rounds of cork in half

Thread the needle with the sewing silk

Tie a knot in the end

Thread a cork and then a bead on the sewing silk, continue with corks and beads until the last half-round is threaded

Tie the ends of the silk together

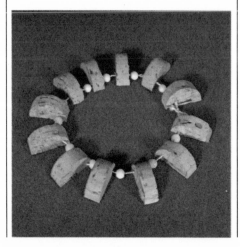

285 Washerwoman

You will need:

A small matchbox, paper, glue, paint, brushes, scissors

What to do:

Cut out the shape shown below and paint it

Fold along the dotted lines

Glue A to the cover of the matchbox

Glue B to the drawer of the matchbox

Open and close the box and the washerwoman will work

15 mm
⅝in

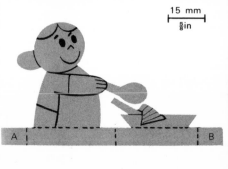

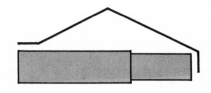

124

286 Ballerina

You will need:

Two corks, a round of cork, 18
pins, paper, paint, scissors, glue,
a hairpin

What to do:

Cut one cork in two and cut a disc
of paper to fit the top of the cork

Push eight pins into each of the
halves of cork as shown in the
figure below (2)

Place the round of cork on top of
one of the cork with pins

Place the paper between them

Push a pin through the paper and
into the cork with pins

Glue the paper to the underside
of the round of cork

Push the free end of the pin into
the whole cork

Push a pin through the other half
of cork with pins

Push this into the side of the
whole cork so that the pins of
each half cork form cogs

Make a handle from the hairpin
and attach it to the side cork

Cut out the dancer and paint her

Make a slit in the round of cork
and place the ballerina in this

Turn the handle and the ballerina
will dance

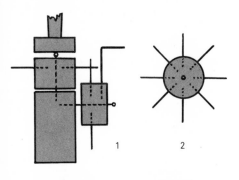

1   2

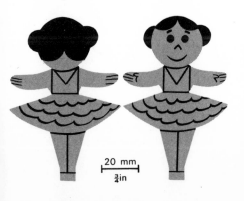

20 mm
¾in

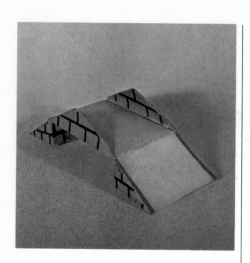

288 Watermill

You will need:

A small box of matches, paper, a round of cork, paint, brushes, glue, scissors, a pin

What to do:

Make a hole in the cover of the matchbox as shown in plan 1

Make 3 slits in the round of cork and push vanes of paper (3) into them

Push the pin through the centre of the cork and place the cork in the matchbox with the pin resting on the cover

Cut out shapes 1 and 2, paint them

Stick 1 to the matchbox cover

Fold 2 along the dotted lines and stick this to the cover so that the ends of the pin are covered

Open and close the matchbox to make the mill wheel move

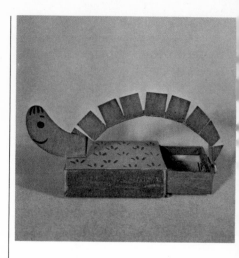

287 Bridge

You will need:

The drawer from a small box of matches, card, paint, glue, brushes, scissors

What to do:

Cut the drawer as shown in the two diagrams below

Open it out and make the roadway of the bridge from paper

Paint the bridge after glueing the roadway in place

289 Green Snake

You will need:

A small matchbox, paper, paint, brushes, glue, scissors

What to do:

Cut out the snake from paper and paint it

Cut along the lines on the back of the snake

Fold along the dotted line

Stick flap A to the matchbox cover

Stick flap B to the matchbox drawer

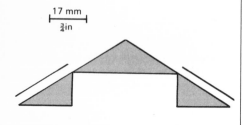

17 mm
³⁄₄in

16 mm
³⁄₄in

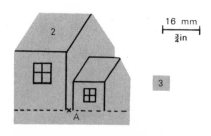

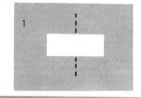

22 mm
⁷⁄₈in

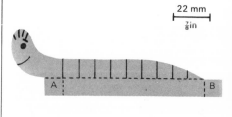

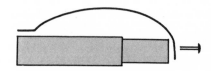

290 Seal

You will need:

A ping-pong ball, light card, paint, brushes, glue, a match

What to do:

Cut out the seal's body and two fins

Stick the fins to the seal

Paint the seal

Paint the ping-pong ball

Stick the match behind the seal's head and attach the ping-pong ball to the end of the match

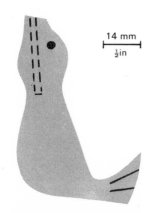

14 mm
½in

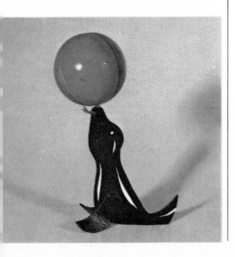

291 White Bird

You will need:

A small matchbox, paper, paint, brushes, glue

What to do:

Cut out the shape below from paper and paint it

Bend along the dotted lines

Make a slit in the matchbox cover and pass flap A through this

Glue the feet to the cover and flap B to the inside of the drawer

20 mm
¾in

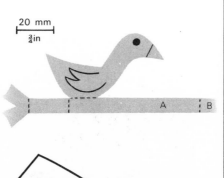

292 Little Fish

You will need:

A matchbox cover, paint, brushes, a wooden peg, a long pin, a small piece of cork

What to do:

Paint the body of the fish on the matchbox sleeve

Paint the rounded tips of the peg bright red

Place the peg in the matchbox and push the pin through the box so that it passes through the wire spiral on the peg's spring

Protect the point of the pin with the small piece of cork

Open and close the peg to make the fishes' mouth move

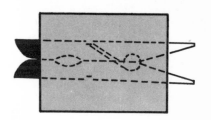

294 Felt Tiger

You will need:
Yellow and black felt, sewing silk, scissors, cotton wool

What to do:
Cut out two body shapes, the tail tuft, the ears twice and several stripes
Sew the body shapes together, inserting cotton-wool as you sew and leaving the legs free
Sew on the ears, tail tuft and stripes
Embroider an eye and whiskers to each side of the head

293 Green Elephant

You will need:
Green and yellow felt, cotton wool, sewing silk, scissors

What to do:
Cut out the body of the elephant twice, the ears twice and the tusks twice
Sew the body pieces together, leaving the legs free
Stuff the body with cotton-wool as you sew
Attach the ears and the tusks
Embroider an eye on the head

295 Felt Giraffe

You will need:
Yellow felt, black felt, sewing silks, cotton-wool, scissors

What to do:
Cut out two body shapes, two ears and two horns
Sew the body shapes together, inserting cotton-wool as you sew and leaving the legs free
Stick black patches to the body
Sew the ears and horns in place

19 mm
¾in

16 mm
¾in

22 mm
1in

296 Eiffel Tower

You will need:

A cork, four matchboxes, paint, glue, brushes, scissors, pin, paper

What to do:

Cut a V shape into three of the matchboxes (see diagram)

Glue the matchboxes together as shown in the photograph

Glue the cork to the top

Make a flag from the paper and the pin

Push it into the cork

Paint the Eiffel tower

297 Roundabout with Birds

You will need:

Card, three corks, 21 pins,
a hairpin, scissors, paint,
brushes, a bead

What to do:

Cut one cork in two

Cut two rounds from the other
cork

Cut two rounds in two and make
the bases for the three birds from
three half rounds

Cut out the birds and paint them

Insert the birds into the bases

Stick pins into the half corks as
shown in figure 1

Join the corks together as
shown in figure 2 with the bead
acting as a bearing for the top
turntable

Make a turning handle for the side
cogs with the hairpin

Turn the handle and the birds will
rotate

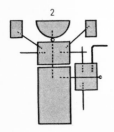

298 Pine Cone Duck

You will need:

A pine cone, three little nails,
a half round of cork, 2 beads, glue

What to do:

Make the beak from 2 nails
pushed into the half round of cork

Stick beads to the head for the
eyes

Attach the head to the cone with
remaining nail

299 Cage Bird

You will need:

Paper, cotton, two matchbox
drawers, paint, scissors, brushes,
glue, wool

What to do:

Cut out two circles of card, each
13cm (5in.) in diameter

Cut out the centre of one of the
circles

Glue the matchbox drawers to the
complete circle

Thread the wool through the ring
and the cage base to make the
bars

Cut out the parts of the little
bird, paint them and slot them
together

Place this inside the cage

Cut out shape 1 and use this as a
ring to hang the cage from

18 mm
¾ in

130

300 Cockerel

You will need:
Card, a hairpin, a half round of cork, paint, brushes

What to do:
Cut out the body of the cockerel from paper
Paint it
Insert it into a slit in the half round of cork
Make the legs from the hairpin
Push the legs into the cork base

17 mm
¾in

301 Pink Pig

You will need:
Card, paint, brushes, scissors

What to do:
Cut out all the shapes and paint them
Assemble the pig by interlocking the slots

20 mm
¾in

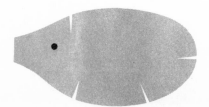

302 Little Birdcage

You will need:
A cork, a large hairpin, red felt, 13 pins, paper, a small curtain ring, paint, glue, brushes

What to do:
Cut the cork into 3 rounds of decreasing size
Make the holder for the cage from the hairpin as shown in the photograph
Anchor the holder in the largest round of cork
Stick this to the paper base
Make the cage from the smaller rounds of cork joined with the pins
Cut out the bird from felt and place it in the cage
Glue the ring to the top of the cage
Hang the cage on its support

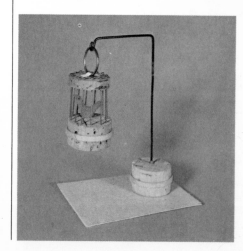

303 Tortoise with a Long Neck

You will need:
A matchbox, paint, brushes

What to do:
Paint the body of the tortoise on the matchbox cover
Paint the head and neck of the tortoise onto the matchbox drawer
Push the drawer out slowly

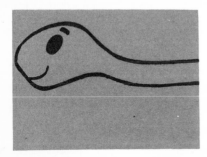

304 Little Duck

You will need:
A matchbox sleeve, paint, brushes, a wooden peg, a long pin, a small piece of cork

What to do:
Paint the duck's head onto the sleeve of the matchbox
Paint the rounded tips of the peg bright yellow
Place the peg in the matchbox and push the pin through the box so that it passes through the wire spiral on the peg's spring
Protect the point of the pin with a small piece of cork
Open and close the peg to make the duck's beak move

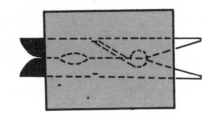

305 Cork Rabbit

You will need:
Two corks, five used matches, four pins, three little nails, three beads, drawing paper, paint, brushes, scissors, felt pen

What to do:
Cut out two ears from the plan below, make two slits in the cork and push the ears into them
Paint the ears blue
Push three small nails into the cork so that they hold the beads in place
Push the pins into the cork to make the whiskers
Push a match into the head of the rabbit
Attach the second cork to this
Push the remaining four matches into the lower cork to make the legs
Draw the mouth onto the upper cork with a felt pen

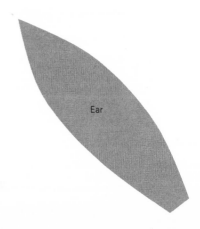

Ear

306 Yellow Giraffe

You will need:
Card, paint, brushes, scissors

What to do:
Cut out all the shapes and paint them

Assemble the giraffe by inter-locking the slots

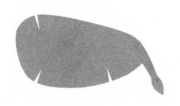

23 mm
1in

307 Rocking Rabbit

You will need:

Stiff drawing paper, cardboard, a cork, a length of wire, 13cm (7¼in.) long, four beads with holes large enough to fit round the wire, two pins, a small nail, an elastic band, glue, scissors, paint, brushes, glue, a small washer, compasses

What to do:

Draw a semi-circle of 12cm (8¾in.) on the drawing paper

Cut it out and roll it into a cone, the base should measure 7½cm (3in.)

Cut out two shapes A from the cardboard

Cut two shapes B and two shapes C (ears and front legs) from the paper

Cut out one shape D (tail) from the paper

Look carefully at the little diagram at the end of these instructions and push the length of wire through the base of the cone, 1cm (⅜in.) from the lower edge

22 mm
1in

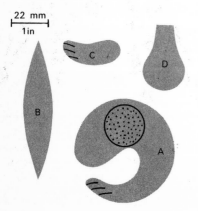

Push a bead onto each end of the wire

Cut two rounds of cork and stick them to the outsides of the back legs

Push the legs onto the ends of the wire and bend the wire ends as shown

Push a pin into each cork round

Thread one end of the elastic through a bead and thread the elastic through the tip of the cone, tie the free end of the elastic to the axle

Stick the tail, the ears and the front legs to the cone

Stick the small washer to the inside of the tail

308 Porcupine

You will need:

A small pine cone, plastic toothpicks, two drawing pins, enamel paint, brush

What to do:

Push the plastic toothpicks into the pine cone, look carefully at the picture and you will see that the toothpicks are pushed in between the little sections of the cone

Push the drawing pins into the cone to make the eyes

Paint the drawing pins white and put a black dot on each one

309 Bengal Tiger

You will need:

Card, paint, brushes, scissors

What to do:

Cut out all the shapes and paint them

Assemble the tiger by interlocking the slots

28 mm
1¼in

310 Tabby Cat

You will need:

Card, paint, brushes, scissors

What to do:

Cut out all the shapes and paint them

Assemble the tabby cat by interlocking the slits

14 mm
½in

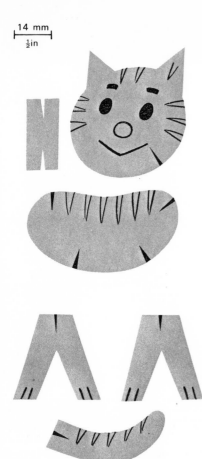

311 Felix the Cat

You will need:

Card, paint, brushes, scissors

What to do:

Cut out all the shapes and paint them

Assemble the pieces by interlocking the slots

22 mm
1in

312 Tropical Fish

You will need:

An elongated light bulb, drawing paper, scissors, glue, enamel paint

What to do:

Cut out two shapes A (tail), one shape B (upper fin) and two shapes C (lower fins)

Glue the tail shapes round the neck of the light bulb

Glue the upper fin into place

Glue the lower fins in place

Paint the fish with enamel paint

16 mm
⅝in

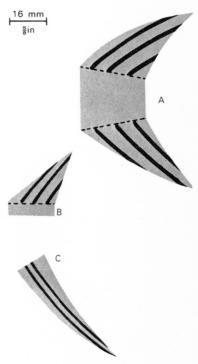

A

B

C

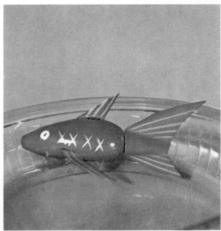

313 Rolling Snail

You will need:

A ping-pong ball, scissors, a sharp knife, paint, brushes, a hairpin, a cork

What to do:

Cut the lower part of a ping-pong ball away

Trim the cork and place it inside the larger part of the ping-pong ball

Cut the hairpin in half and push one half through the ping-pong ball, through the cork and out through the ping-pong ball again so that the cork acts as a little wheel

Cut out the head and tail and bend them along the dotted lines

Stick them to the ping-pong ball

Paint the snail

314 Bird and Chicks

You will need:

A small matchbox, drawing paper, paints, brushes, scissors, glue

What to do:

Cut out the bird and her chicks from drawing paper

Fold along the dotted lines

Stick A to the sleeve of the matchbox

Stick B to the drawer of the matchbox

Paint the bird, the chicks and the matchbox

15 mm
½in

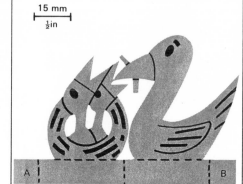

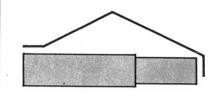

315 Croaking Toad

You will need:

A ping-pong ball, a pin, drawing paper, paint, brush, scissors, pliers

What to do:

Cut the ping-pong ball into two unequal parts

Attach the smaller part to the larger part (see diagram) with the pin, by pushing the pin through both parts and bending the tip of the pin over to hold it in place

Cut out the legs from paper

Stick the legs in place

Paint the toad

The toad will croak if you scratch the inner part of the ping-pong ball with your fingernail

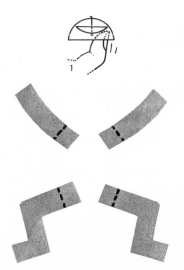

316 Crocodile Letter Holder

You will need:

Green felt, yellow felt, black felt, a peg, sewing thread and a needle, scissors, two small curtain rings, two beads, glue, cotton wool

What to do:

Cut out two pieces A, one from green felt and one from yellow felt

Cut out two pieces B from black felt and sew them together along the short straight side

Cut out three strips of black felt, these are for the eyebrows and the band between the eyes

Embroider the zig-zag down the centre of the green piece of felt

Sew the eyebrows and the rings on the green felt, join the rings with a band of black felt and sew the beads on for the eyes

Join the two halves of the crocodile and as you sew them together, stuff the body with cotton wool

When you reach the head, sew the mouth piece in, inserting the peg as you sew

34 mm
1⅜in

Place the donkey's head behind the body and push the little nail through holes A and B

Protect the sharp end of the nail with a small piece of cork

Open and close the peg and the donkey will nod his head

317 Moving Donkey

You will need:

A peg, a large hairpin, pliers, a drawing pin, a small piece of cork, a pin, a little nail, card, paint, brushes, scissors

What to do:

Cut out the head and body of the donkey from card

Pierce them at A, B and C

Paint them

Bend flap D back and stick it to one side of the peg

Cut the hair pin in half and bend one half into the shape shown in E

Attach the looped end of the wire to the lower part of the peg with the drawing pin

Push the hooked end of the wire through hole C in the donkey's neck

34 mm
1⅜in

318 Snail Picture

You will need:

Two dried autumn leaves, card, paper, scissors, paints, brushes, glue, varnish, a sheet of card 300cm (12in.) square

What to do:

Paint the sheet of card with a plain colour

Stick the two leaves onto it

Cut out a little snail from the card

Paint it

Stick the snail onto the leaves

Varnish everything

319 Red Fighting Fish

You will need:

A cork, thin card, paint, brushes, glue, scissors, two small beads, two small nails which will pass through the beads, sharp knife, varnish

What to do:

Cut out the fins from card

Paint them

Cut a notch in the cork to make the fish's mouth

Make slits in the cork for the tail and the fins

Push the tail and the fins into the slits and glue them

Fix the beads to the fish's head with the small nails

Paint and varnish the fish

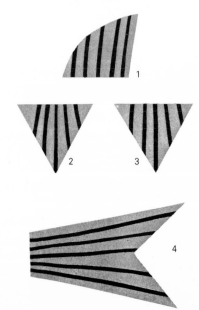

320 Camel

You will need:

Card, scissors, paint, brushes

What to do:

Cut out all the shapes and paint them

Assemble the pieces by interlocking them at the slots

26 mm
1in

321 Dragonfly

You will need:

Four sycamore fruits, a cork, card, glue, a wooden base, a small nail, paint, brushes, scissors, four pins

What to do:

Cut out and paint the body of the dragonfly

Attach the wings with pins

Push the nail into the cork and glue the underside of the body to the nail

Stick the cork to the wooden base

322 Little Blue Donkey

You will need:

Card, paint, brushes, scissors

What to do:

Cut out all the shapes and paint them

Assemble the donkey by slotting the parts together so that the slits interlock

25 mm
1in

323 Tulip Jewellery Holder

You will need:

Card, drawing paper, red felt, glue, scissors, paint, brushes, two small curtain rings, thin red string, cotton wool

What to do:

Cut shapes 1 and 2 from card and shape 3 from drawing paper

Cover shape 3 with red felt

Paint shape 1 as shown in the picture

Bend shape 3 along the dotted lines and stick A and B to shape 1

Place shape 2 in the semi-circular hole at the base of the jewellery holder

32 mm
1¼in

Tie two curtain rings to the thin string and hang the jewellery holder from them where marked (C and D)

Loosely fill the holder with cotton wool and jewels

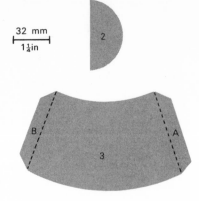

32 mm
1¼in

324 Ostrich

You will need:

Half a walnut shell, a round of cork, two large hairpins, glue, pliers

What to do:

Cut the round of cork in half

Cover one half with the half walnut shell and glue the shell in place

Cut one hair pin in half and bend each lower half into a right angle

Push the right angled wire into the half cork to make the legs

Cut the other hairpin in half

Make the neck and the beak with these halves

Push the neck and the beak into the half round of cork

Draw an eye on each side of the head

325 Kitten with a Ball

You will need:

Two ping-pong balls, a cork, three hairpins, four beads which will thread on the hairpins, a drawing pin, a used match, drawing paper, paint, varnish, brushes, scissors, glue

What to do:

Open the hairpins

Push one of them through one ping-pong ball and bend the protruding ends of the wire back and push them into the end of the cork

Bend another hairpin into a flattened U shape and thread four beads on it

Push the ends of the wire into the cork to make the back legs

Push a match into the second ping-pong ball to make the head and neck

Push the neck into the cork

Push the drawing pin into the head to make the nose

Stick two little triangles of drawing paper to the top of the head to make the ears

Paint the head and balloon

326 Little Mermaid

You will need:

A pine cone, a ping-pong ball, glue, a round piece of wood, green felt, yellow felt, drawing paper, a length of wire 8cm (3¼in.) long, paints, brushes, a small hammer, scissors

What to do:

Attach the ping-pong ball to the pine cone by gently hammering the wire through the cone and pushing the ping-pong ball onto the other end

Cover the wood with a round of green felt

Make a hole in the round piece of wood and push the other end of the wire into this

Cut out the three shapes shown below from drawing paper

Curve the front of the body round and stick it to the pine cone

Stick piece B to the back of the body

Stick the tail to the pine cone

Paint the mermaid

Cut the yellow felt into strips and stick the strips to the ping-pong ball to make the hair

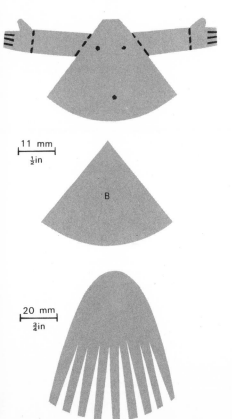

11 mm
½in

B

20 mm
¾in

Stuff the body of the frog with cotton wool

Insert the peg into the frog with the jaws of the peg towards the mouth

Start to sew the inside-mouth gusset into place, stuffing the frog with more cotton wool and manoeuvring the peg into place

Sew the buttons on for the eyes

327 Frog Letter Holder

You will need:

Red felt, sewing thread, needle, peg, scissors, a peg, cotton wool, two buttons

What to do:

Cut out two frog shapes (A) and two gussets (B)

Sew the gussets together along their longest edge

Sew three lines of chain stitch down the centre of one of the frog pieces

Sew the frog pieces together, leaving the head unsewn

328 Millipede

You will need:

Two corks, a large hairpin, three little beads, three nails which will go through the beads, fourteen pins, paint, a sharp knife, brushes, varnish

What to do:

Cut each of the corks into four rounds

Open the hairpin completely.

Push the hairpin wire through the centre of each round of cork

Push two pins into each of the seven cork rounds which make the body

Push two pins into the head to make the antennae

Fix the beads to the head with the small nails to make the eyes and nose

Paint and varnish the millipede

329 Kangaroo Needlecase

You will need:

Black felt, red felt, sewing thread, scissors, a packet of needles, cotton wool

What to do:

Cut out two kangaroo shapes from black felt and one pocket shape from red felt

Sew the kangaroo shapes together round the edges, as you sew, stuff the kangaroo with cotton wool

Sew the lower three sides of the pocket to the kangaroo's tummy

Embroider the kangaroo's eye

Put the packet of needles into the pocket

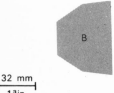

32 mm
1⅜in

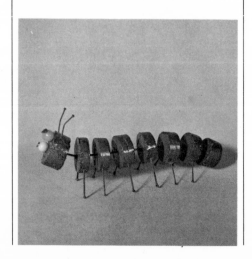

24 mm
1in

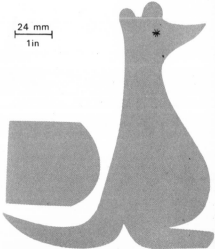

330 Giraffe Scissors Case

You will need:

Red felt, sewing thread, needle, scissors, cotton wool

What to do:

Cut out two giraffe shapes and sew them together. Sew first along the dotted line on the plan (this makes the pocket for the scissors)

Sew the shapes together around the edges leaving the top of the pocket open and inserting a little cotton wool to stuff the giraffe

Embroider an eye on the giraffe

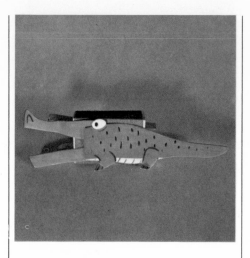

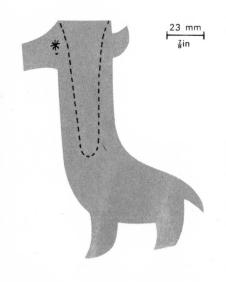

23 mm
⅞ in

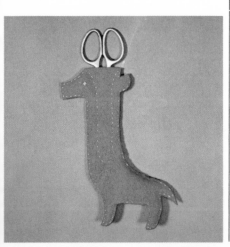

331 Crocodile

You will need:

A small matchbox, drawing paper, glue, a peg, paint, brushes, a pair of scissors

What to do:

Cut out shapes A, B and C from drawing paper and paint them

Stick parts A and B to the tapered side of the peg, A to the upper part and B to the lower part. Only glue them at the part marked with lines on the pattern

Slip the peg inside the matchbox cover but allow the unglued ends of A and B to stay outside the matchbox cover

Stick part C onto the matchbox cover being careful not to glue it to A and B

If you pinch the tapered ends of the peg the crocodile will open and shut his jaws

17 mm
¾ in

332 Blue Elephant

You will need:

Cardboard, scissors, paint, brushes, varnish

What to do:

Cut out all the parts of the elephant from cardboard and paint them

Varnish them

Assemble the elephant by pushing the parts together so that the slits interlock

26 mm
1 in

Make a slit in the round of cork and push the little bird into it

When the drawer of the matchbox is pushed in and out the bird will rock

333 Green Bird

You will need:

A small matchbox, a round of cork, drawing paper, glue, scissors, paint, brushes, a long pin

What to do:

Cut out shapes A and B from the drawing paper

Paint them

Place piece B onto the matchbox cover and cut a hole in the cover to match the hole in piece B

Push the pin through the round of cork and put the cork into the closed matchbox with the pin resting on the cover at the sides of the hole

Stick piece B in place to hold the pin steady

334 Rocking Chicken

You will need:

A wooden cotton reel, sawn in half lengthways, a hacksaw, card, paint, brushes, glue, scissors

What to do:

Cut out the chicken from the card, and paint and varnish it

Make a slit in the bobbin with the hacksaw and push the base of the chicken into it

18 mm
¾in

335 Pecking Hen

You will need:

A small matchbox, drawing paper, scissors, paint, brushes, glue, some tiny seeds

What to do:

Cut out the farmer and his hen

Fold them along the dotted lines

Stick the rectangle of paper which is the grass to the matchbox cover

Stick part A of the strip beneath the bird to the matchbox cover at B and stick part C of the strip beneath the bird to the drawer of the box

16 mm
⅝in

17 mm
¾in

A

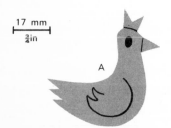

B

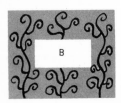

B

16 mm
⅝in

Paint a little clear glue on the grass and sprinkle the seeds on it

Push the matchbox drawer in and out and the bird will peck

336 Egg Cosy

You will need:

Blue felt, red embroidery silk, needle, scissors

What to do:

Cut out two triangles of blue felt

Sew them together to half way up each side and then across the triangle

Make a little tassel for each point by knotting a bunch of short lengths of embroidery silk together and sewing them to each point

17 mm
¾in

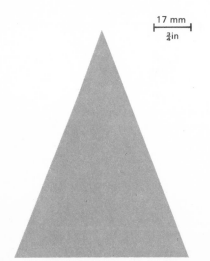

337 Jumping Frog

You will need:

Two pegs, drawing paper, scissors, paint, brushes, glue

What to do:

Cut the frog shape out of drawing paper

Paint it

Stick it to one side of the peg

To make the frog jump, push a half peg in between the rounded halves of the peg with the frog. Gently push the 'frog-peg' off the half peg and as the jaws snap shut the frog will leap forward

338 Blue Whale

You will need:

Cardboard, blue felt, pink felt, needle and thread, a button, 13 pins, scissors, glue

What to do:

Cut out the whale's shape (1) from blue felt and card

Cut the mouth (2) from pink felt

Cut the fin (3) from blue felt

Sew the button to the whale to make the eye

Sew the fin to the whale

Sew the mouth to the whale

Stick the felt whale to the card whale

Stick the pins into the whale's jaws

Cut out piece (4) from card and bend it along the dotted line

Stick A to the back of the whale so that the card strip holds the whale upright

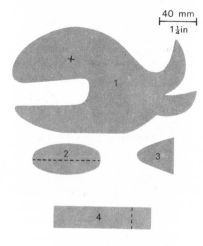

40 mm
1¼in

339 Rocking Donkey

You will need:

A small matchbox, drawing paper, a round of cork, a long pin, scissors, paint, brushes, glue

What to do:

Cut out shapes A and B from the drawing paper

Place B on the matchbox cover and cut a hole in the cover to match the hole in the paper

Push the pin (shortened if necessary) through the cork round

Place the cork in the matchbox so that the pin rests on each side of the hole on the cover

Stick piece B over the matchbox sleeve so that it holds the pin in place

Make a slit in the cork and push the donkey into it

13 mm
½in

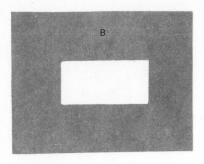

Paint the model
Open and close the matchbox to make the donkey rock

342 Hopping Bird

You will need:
A peg, drawing paper, paint, brushes, scissors, glue

What to do:
Cut out shapes A and B from the drawing paper
Paint them
Stick the bird to the top half of the peg and the grass to the lower half of the peg
Make the bird hop by opening and closing the peg .

341 Flying Bird

You will need:
A small matchbox, drawing paper, glue, a paper fastener, scissors, paint, brushes

What to do:
Cut out shapes 1 and 2 from the drawing paper
Paint them
Bend them along the dotted lines
Stick the wings to the band at the base of the bird's body
Roll the wings round a crayon to curve them
Stick A to the sleeve of the matchbox
Make a small slit at the front of the matchbox sleeve
Push the band through this slit and glue B to the inside of the drawer
Push the paper fastener into the front of the matchbox drawer to make a handle
Push the drawer in and out to make the bird move

340 Cat Game

You will need:
The drawer of a little box of matches, drawing paper, two drawing pins, scissors, paint, brushes, Cellophane paper

What to do:
Cut a rectangle of paper to fit into the matchbox drawer
Draw the face of a cat onto it (see the picture)
Stick the drawing to the matchbox drawer
Put the drawing pins into the matchbox drawer
Cover the open side of the matchbox with cellophane
Shake the box and try to get the pins to cover the eye shapes

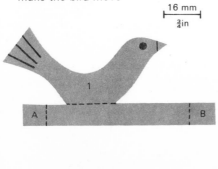

16 mm
¾ in

147

344 Floating Island

You will need:
Drawing paper, a half-round of cork, a nail, scissors, paint, brushes

What to do:
Cut out the island shape from the drawing paper
Paint and varnish it
Make a slit in the flat side of the half-round of cork and stick the base of the island into it
Push the nail into the curved side of the cork
Place the cork in water and the island will float

343 Swimming Duck

You will need:
Drawing paper, a half-round of cork, a nail, scissors, paint, brushes

What to do:
Cut out the duck's body from the drawing paper
Paint and varnish it
Make a slit in the cork and stick the base of the duck's body into it
Push the nail into the curved side of the cork
Place the cork in water and the duck will float

345 Spaniel

You will need:
One large light bulb, two smaller, oval bulbs, Plasticine, enamel paint, a piece of board

What to do:
Make three balls of Plasticine, stick one to the board and push the neck of the larger bulb into it
Stick the other balls of Plasticine to the top of the bulb and stick the two smaller bulbs to these
Paint the features of the spaniel on the larger bulb
Take care when handling the light bulbs, they are fragile

346 Glass Duck

You will need:

One large and one small light bulb,
Plasticine, enamel paint, brushes,
a piece of board

What to do:

Make two balls of Plasticine and
stick one to the board

Stick the side of the larger bulb to
the Plasticine

Stick the other ball of Plasticine to
the other side of the larger bulb
and stick the smaller bulb to this

Paint the duck's wing on the
larger bulb and its eye and eye-
brow on the smaller bulb

Take care then handling light
bulbs, they are fragile

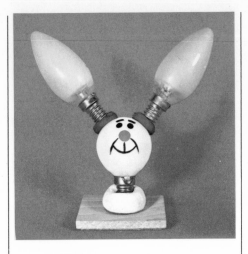

347 Glass Rabbit

You will need:

Three light bulbs (two candle-
flame bulbs and one round bulb),
Plasticine, enamel paint, a piece of
board

What to do:

Make three balls of Plasticine,
stick one to the board and push
the neck of the round bulb into it

Gently stick the other two balls of
Plasticine to the top of the round
bulb and push the necks of the
oval light bulbs into them

Paint the rabbit's face onto the
round bulb

Take care when handling the light
bulbs, they are fragile

348 Auguste the Clown

You will need:

Two old light bulbs, one large and
one small, Plasticine, enamel paint,
brushes, a piece of board

What to do:

Make two balls of Plasticine, stick
one to the board and push the
neck of the larger light bulb into it

Carefully stick the other ball of
Plasticine to the side of the larger
light bulb and push the neck of
the smaller light bulb into it

Paint the features onto the bulbs

Take care when handling the light
bulbs, they are fragile

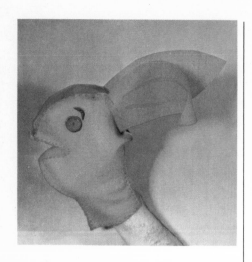

349 Rabbit Puppet

You will need:

A large piece of orange felt, a smaller piece of pink felt, scraps of blue and black felt, orange sewing thread, a needle, scissors, drawing paper, paint, brushes

What to do:

Cut out two head shapes (A), one gusset (B) and one gusset (C), from the orange felt and one inside mouth piece (D) from the pink felt

Cut out two ears (E) from the drawing paper and paint them orange

Cut out two circles of blue for the eyes and two semi-circular curves for the eyebrows

Sew gusset (C) between the two head shapes from (F) to (G) (see head pattern)

30 mm
1⅛in

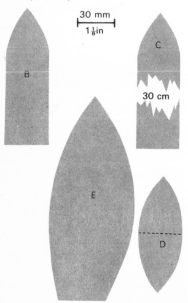

Sew gusset (B) between the two head shapes from (H) to (J)

Sew piece (D) into the mouth opening

Sew the eyes and eyebrows onto the puppet

Sew the ears onto the puppet

Make whiskers with embroidery thread

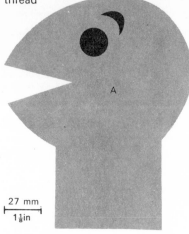

27 mm
1⅛in

350 Fish made with Leaves

You will need:

A large beech leaf, five smaller leaves, glue, scissors, a piece of felt 15cm (6in.) square, a piece of stiff card 15cm (6in.) square

What to do:

Cut the mouth of the fish from the big leaf

Stick the square of felt to the square of card

Stick the big leaf to the centre of the felt and the smaller leaves round it as shown in the picture

Make the eye from either a scrap of felt or a coloured bead

351 White Rabbit

You will need:

Drawing paper, paints, brushes, scissors

What to do:

Cut out the rabbit from the drawing paper

Paint it

Put your index and middle finger through the holes to make the ears

32 mm
1¼in

150

352 Fish in a Bowl

You will need:

Cardboard, an egg which has been blown, scissors, paint, brushes, glue

What to do:

Cut out a bowl shape (A) and two shapes (B)

Stick the egg into the hole in the bowl

Push the two supports (B) into the base of the bowl

Paint the bowl, the egg and the supports

Varnish them

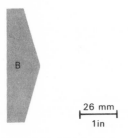

26 mm
1 in

353 Thimble-holder

You will need:

Blue felt, sewing thread to match, needle, cotton wool, embroidery silk, scissors, thimble

What to do:

Cut out two camel shapes from the blue felt

Sew them together round the edges

As you sew, push cotton wool into the shape

Embroider the eye with embroidery silk

Put the thimble onto the camel's hump

18 mm
¾ in

354 Jumping Frog

You will need:

A small box of matches, a used match, a paper fastener, drawing paper, glue, scissors, paint, brushes

What to do:

Cut out the frog shape from the drawing paper

Bend it along the dotted lines

Stick the feet to the sleeve of the matchbox

Attach the part marked with a cross to the drawer of the matchbox

Push the match between the drawer and the sleeve of the matchbox

Paint the matchbox and the frog

If you push the matchbox drawer gently in and out the frog will hop and make a croaking noise

18 mm
¾ in

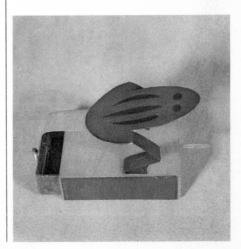

356 Little Man

You will need:

Drawing paper, paint, brushes, scissors

What to do:

Cut out the little man from the drawing paper

Paint him

Put your index and middle finger through the holes in the little man and make him wave his arms about

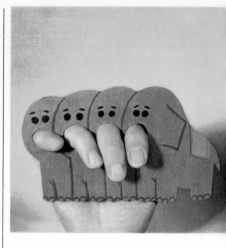

355 Trumpeting Elephant

You will need:

Drawing paper, paints, brushes, scissors

What to do:

Cut out the elephant from drawing paper

Paint it

Put your index finger through the hole in the elephant's head and make him wave his trunk about

25 mm
1 in

357 Elephants

You will need:

Drawing paper, paint, brushes, scissors

What to do:

Cut out the row of elephants from the drawing paper

Paint them

Put all four fingers of one hand through the row of holes

23 mm
$\frac{7}{8}$in

31 mm
$1\frac{1}{4}$in

152

358 Snail

You will need:

Drawing paper, paint, brushes, scissors

What to do:

Cut out the snail from drawing paper

Paint it

Put your index and middle finger through the top holes and your thumb through the lower hole

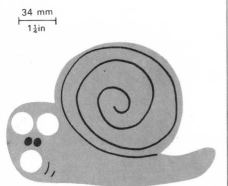

34 mm
1¼in

359 Crowing Cockerel

You will need:

Drawing paper, paint, brushes, scissors

What to do:

Cut out the cockerel's shape from the drawing paper

Paint it

Put your index finger and thumb through the holes in the cockerel's head and open and close them to make the cock seem as if it is crowing

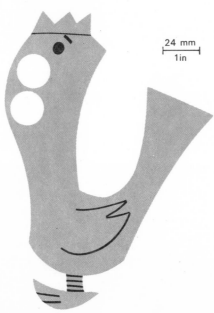

24 mm
1in

360 Duck Puppet

You will need:

Drawing paper, paint, brushes, scissors

What to do:

Cut out the duck's shape from the drawing paper

Paint it

Put your index finger through the hole in the duck's head and wiggle it about

27 mm
1⅛in

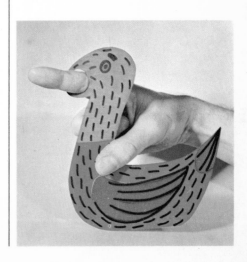

361 Little Duck

You will need:

A thick round of cork and a thin round of cork, a used match, drawing paper, scissors, glue, paint, brushes

What to do:

Cut off a quarter of the thick round of cork – this is for the body of the duck

Cut the thin round of cork in half – this is for the feet

Cut the match in half and attach the feet to the body with the matchstick halves

Cut out the two parts of the duck (head and tail) from drawing paper

Cut slits in the cork body and insert the head and tail

Paint the little duck

362 Emperor Penguin

You will need:

A ping-pong ball, a cork and a round cut from a cork, drawing paper, a used match, glue, scissors, paint, brushes

What to do:

Push the match into the ping-pong ball and into the cork

Cut out the beak (1), the tail (2) and a pair of wings (3) from drawing paper

Bend the beak and stick it to the ping-pong ball

Stick the wings and the tail to the cork

Cut the round of cork into halves and stick these to the base of the cork to make the feet

Paint the penguin

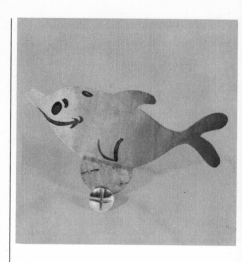

363 Dolphin

You will need:

A half-round of cork, two small screws, drawing paper, paint, brushes, scissors

What to do:

Cut out the dolphin shape from drawing paper

Paint it

Cut a slit in the half-round of cork and push the dolphin's tummy into it

Glue it in place

Screw two small screws into the sides of the cork

Place the model in water and pull the nose gently, let it go and it will move gently in the water

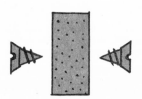

364 Hedgehog
Pin-cushion

You will need:

Yellow felt, yellow sewing thread and a needle, cotton wool, scissors, pins

What to do:

Cut out two hedgehog shapes from felt

Sew them together round the edges with matching sewing cotton

As you sew them together, insert a little cotton wool from time to time

Fasten off securely

Embroider an eye on each side

Stick the hedgehog full of pins

365 Painted Box

You will need:

A cardboard box, patterned wrapping paper, glue, scissors, paint, brushes

What to do:

Paint the box all over with a plain colour

Cut out motifs from the wrapping paper

Stick these motifs to the box or paint your own design onto the box

Varnish the box

. . . and this is the extra one for Leap Year.

Trumpet

You will need:

A wooden cotton reel, an old pencil which will fit into the hole in the cotton reel, a large hairpin, paint, brushes, glue, pliers, a hacksaw, two red tassels, a gimlet

What to do:

Cut the cotton reel in half

Push and stick the pencil into the hole in the half cotton reel

Make two holes in the pencil with a gimlet

Bend the hairpin into the shape shown in the picture and push each end into a hole and glue it

Tie the tassels to the hairpin

Paint the trumpet

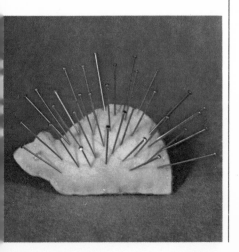

INDEX

STOCKISTS LIST

Haberdashery Counters
Scissors, needles, pins, beads, bodkins, darning
needles, hairpins, sewing thread, wools,
embroidery silks, felt, safety pins, clothes-pegs

Stationers
Card, paper, graph paper, string, glue, rubber
solution glue, paper fasteners, crayons, felt
pens, varnish, pencils, ruler, compasses,
rubber bands

Ironmongers
Nails, screws, a gimlet, hacksaw, light
hammers, pliers, craft knives, fuse wire,
clothes-pegs

Art Shops
Paints, brushes, varnishes, crayons and felt
pens, card, paper, graph paper, modelling clay,
glues, drawing pins, compasses

General Stores
Ping-pong balls, drinking straws, matchboxes,
cotton reels, light bulbs, scissors

Try asking the sewing departments at school
to save their cotton reels.

Ask your local restaurant to save corks.

Ask everyone to save matchboxes, small boxes,
used matches, pill tubes and toothpaste caps.